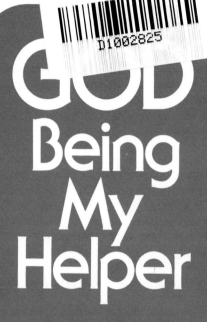

GOD
Being
My
Helper

Ralph A. Herring

Copyright 1955
BROADMAN PRESS
Nashville, Tennessee

ISBN: 0-8054-1925-X

4219-25

Dewey Decimal Classification: 231.3
Library of Congress catalog card number: 55-14629
Printed in the United States of America

CONTENTS

BROADMAN PRESS · **Nashville, Tennessee**

FOREWORD

"May I help you?"

Turning, I looked into the kind face of a saleslady who had come upon me fumbling in a pile of goods on a counter. There was a suggestion of rebuke in her voice, but to me it brought welcome relief. It was bargain day, and I had been assigned the responsibility of purchasing some garments for my small son.

"Just a matter of a few minutes," I had thought, as I eased my Model T into a dubious berth along a curb marked with yellow. But joining in the shoppers' scramble for bargains, I began to be tormented by visions of a parking ticket which would more than offset any advantage gained by a marked-down price tag.

But help had come, and in a moment, the purchase complete, I was on my way back to the car and on home without further difficulty.

"May I help you?" Across the years this incident has become a parable to me. Again and again the searching

query has brought to sharp focus my greatest weakness—
and, I am persuaded, the weakness of most Christians.
Maddened by frustrations in life's scramble for bargains,
confused and fretted by assignments for which I am ill
fitted or disinclined, I am frequently startled to hear God's
voice within asking, "May I help you?" Oftentimes there
is rebuke in it, I must confess, for I am prone to rush in
without recognizing the Helper at my side. But always
there is relief, for mine is ever the place of need.

The biggest problem God faces must be the task of
helping us without hurting us. Recognizing this difficulty,
we have a way of saying, "God helps those who help themselves." But to help one's self may be the most offensive
form of egotism and arrogance. Human nature being
what it is, how can God help us without confirming the
selfishness of our own choices and spoiling us forever? On
the other hand, how can he help us without stifling our
initiative and pauperizing all that marks us as created in
his own image?

Social workers and economists with their welfare states,
psychologists, doctors, teachers, preachers, lawyers, parents
—all are faced with this problem. It would seem that the
world is divided between those who need help and those
who are able to give it and would be happy in so doing.
But what kind of help, on whose terms, when, how?

God's answer to this problem is personal, for in the final
analysis the need is personal. This matter of giving and
receiving help is so delicately balanced, so intricately
woven with the welfare of all concerned, that it could be
dispensed on no other plane. He himself is the answer, his
Spirit, our Helper.

My purpose is to show how God's help becomes avail

able to us. The simple procedure will be to visit the different points of need in Christian experience and to watch him at work there, for at no other place can help be more readily evaluated. On the principle that "a friend in need is a friend indeed," the Holy Spirit shows himself our supreme Friend. Where our need is the greatest, his ministry will be most plainly evident and most sincerely appreciated.

But there is a certain hesitancy in speaking about one's innermost needs which we all respect. For that reason, although I am a preacher by calling, I have not often preached these messages. Many times, however, in smaller groups where there was a heart-hunger to learn more of the ways of the Spirit, I have talked about the unfailing help and victory which God supplies at the time and place of need.

Indeed, so often have I given this witness that now the relation of these experiences seems more a spiritual autobiography than anything else. I have lived with these truths through the greater portion of my ministry. They have meant increasingly more to me with the passing years. Although I have not mastered them, I have come to know their value by experience. I have written much as I have spoken on the occasions mentioned above, and with the same purpose—to show the amazing adequacy of that help which God supplies to our every need through his own indwelling Spirit.

Note: All biblical quotations are from the American Standard Version unless otherwise indicated.

I

The Divine Executive

To the early Christians the presence of the Holy Spirit was life's supreme reality. The firsthandedness of their witness, so refreshing to the reader of the New Testament, can be explained only in the light of their experience at Pentecost. The Comforter had come. He was their silent Partner, their ever-present Friend, their unfailing Source of inspiration and power. Particularly is this evident in the book designated, "The Acts of the Apostles." Frequently referred to as "The Acts of the Holy Spirit," it reveals him carrying into effect through the lives of the apostles and others "all that Jesus began to do and to teach" (Acts 1:1).

But the emphasis on the Holy Spirit found in Acts comes as no surprise to the reader of the Gospels. It is a definite reflection of the teaching and the attitude of Jesus himself. During the first portion of his ministry he appears to have concentrated his efforts upon the revelation of his own identity as the Son of God. For this reason, with evident joy and satisfaction, he hailed Peter's affirmation, "Thou art the Christ, the Son of the living God" (Matt. 16:16). A crisis had been reached with that magnificent declaration. At last they knew who he was!

From this stage in the course of their instruction he passed on to another which came to its culmination in the upper room. They had come to know him; they must come to know the Father. The Fourth Gospel more particularly reveals the concern which became a burning passion with Jesus as the time drew near when he was to be taken from them. On the night in which he was betrayed John tells us that Jesus spoke more and more intimately of the Father. His progress was reflected in Philip's earnest cry, "Lord, show us the Father, and it sufficeth us" (John 14:8). We can be grateful for Philip's seeming dullness. It drew from the lips of Jesus his most revealing statement on the nature of God: "He that hath seen me hath seen the Father" (v. 9).

This satisfying answer marks the transition to another stage in the revelation which the Son of God had come to make. The disciples were now prepared to learn more about the third person of the Godhead, the Holy Spirit. From this point, both in the upper room and through the forty days prior to his ascension, much of our Lord's conversation centers upon that *Other* One whose presence was to be of supreme importance in the lives of his followers. "I will pray the Father," said Jesus, "and he shall give you *another* Comforter, that he may be with you for ever, even the Spirit of truth: whom the world cannot receive; for it beholdeth him not, neither knoweth him: ye know him; for he abideth with you, and shall be in you" (John 14: 16–17).

The significance of the word translated "another" is of

utmost importance. In the Greek it is *allos,* not *heteros;* "another" one, not a "different" one. According to Jesus, there is the Father, the Son, and *One Other*—distinct, but not different—the Holy Spirit. It is *this distinction* within the Godhead to which I direct your attention in this opening chapter. We shall see how the distinction may be traced not only in the persons of the Trinity but also in the office and procedures of each.

A DISTINCTION IN PERSON

The Holy Spirit is a person just as truly as the Father and the Son are persons. These three are co-equal from eternity. This is easy to say, and many will doubtless give their ready assent to it as a statement of faith. But our problem lies deeper. The attitude of thousands of Christians indicates that however readily they may accept the doctrine of the Trinity, in actual experience the Holy Spirit as a person means very little to them. For such, the sense of his reality is weakened by disturbing speculation as to how one God could be Father, Son, and Holy Spirit. Instead of pressing on in faith to enjoy the revelation God has given of himself, they hedge away from the intellectual difficulty of such a concept.

Actually, however, we should not stumble at the fact that we cannot completely understand God. We do not completely understand ourselves, for that matter. A husband may not fully understand his wife, yet he finds his relationship with her all the sweeter and more alluring because of the unfathomable mystery of womanhood. If this be true on the human level, how much more on the divine? Instead of being dismayed, the heart of man will rather be drawn upward and onward by the infinite God whose disclosures of his divine nature challenge, even as they exceed, the fondest reaches of human imagination. Proving through his own experience what God has been pleased to reveal of himself through the Scriptures, the believer will then know (though he may not be able to explain it always to others or even to himself) that God is one and at the same time three persons: Father, Son, and Holy Spirit.

The personality of the Holy Spirit is strikingly emphasized through the use of pronouns in the New Testament. As many readers may be aware, the Greek word for *spirit* is in the neuter gender. The rules of grammar, therefore, require that pronouns and adjectives referring to it be neuter also. But in a number of instances the personality of the Spirit is so strongly felt that contrary to the niceties of grammar, the neuter antecedent is represented by a masculine pronoun. Such is the case in John 14:26 and, more clearly still, in John 16:13 which I quote: "Howbeit when he [*ekeinos,* masculine], the Spirit [*pneuma,* neuter] of truth, is come he shall guide you into all the truth." Dr. A. T. Robertson, in his great *Grammar of the Greek New Testament,* discusses both of these verses and says concerning the latter, "It is more evident, therefore, in this passage that John is insisting on the personality of the Holy Spirit, when the grammatical gender so easily called for (the use of the neuter) *ekeino.*" Thus the Spirit of God is vastly more than an "influence" or a "power," and the terms which we use in speaking of him should reflect our appreciation of this truth.

As a matter of fact, nobody likes to be referred to as "it." I remember from my boyhood days as a son of missionary parents in China that to address someone in such a fashion constituted almost their supreme insult, and in our land also it is clearly resented. Early in my experience as a pastor I made a call in a home which had just been gladdened by the arrival of a baby boy. I had been told the gender of the new addition, but for the moment it had slipped my memory. Being a single man in those days, this did not seem to me a matter of great consequence! During the course of my conversation I employed the only fitting word I knew whereby to cover my uncertainty and inquired, "How is it getting along?" The little mother immediately challenged my disrespect. "I'll have you to know, young man," she said indignantly, "my little son is no *it*. He is the finest little boy in all the world!" I stood corrected, and have carried the lesson with me ever since.

If you have been insufficiently impressed with the personal worth of the great and loving Holy Spirit, or if your conception of him is so confused that he means little more than an influence, or a vague doctrine, I challenge you to open your mind and heart right now to the truth that he is a *person*—as much a person and as real a person as the Son of God our Saviour, or as our Heavenly Father himself.

A further example of the way in which the pronouns of the New Testament teach the personality of the Holy Spirit is the use of the first personal pronoun. Psychologists designate the very center and essence of personality by the term *ego,* which is, of course, simply a transliteration of the Greek first personal pronoun "I." When it occurs in that language, it is chiefly for emphasis. One of the rare instances in which the Holy Spirit refers thus to himself is in Acts 10:20. Peter was in a quandary about accepting the invitation to the home of the Gentile, Cornelius. The Spirit commands: "Arise, and get thee down, and go with them, nothing doubting: for I [*ego*] have sent them." Who but a person could thus speak? And who but the sovereign God would speak with such authority? Peter's immediate obedience and the results which followed leave no doubt about the answer.

Scripture attributes the qualities generally regarded as characteristics of personality—intellect, emotion, and will —to the Spirit of God. Paul says in Ephesians 4:30, "Grieve not the Holy Spirit." This is the language of emotion, for only love can grieve. Nothing so hurts a lover's feelings as to be unappreciated or ignored. Any sin, of course, grieves the Holy Spirit, but this supremely —that he should be utterly and completely ignored, and that by those who profess to be his servants. It is a wicked thing that we do to grieve the Spirit in this manner! We may be sure he feels it keenly, although with amazing love he continues his ministry in our behalf. He has come to sanctify our emotions, bringing in, by his own rich and tender compassion, the love, joy, and peace (Gal. 5:22) which are the first fruits of a well-balanced emotional life.

Another trait of personality is intelligence. Every work of the Spirit is marked in Scripture by infinite wisdom. The stamp of his intellect is upon all that he does. His decisions are infallible. After long hours of deliberation upon a problem that threatened to split the church and fetter the gospel with the bonds of Jewish legalism, the church at Jerusalem introduced their conclusion in this manner: "It *seemed good* to the Holy Spirit and to us" (Acts 15:28). Note the order.

The Spirit also teaches: "But the Comforter, even the Holy Spirit, whom the Father will send in my name, he shall teach you all things" (John 14:26). And what a teacher he is! When I am discouraged by my own dullness, I find comfort in the thought that he is a teacher of infinite skill and patience. He will cause me to know if I really want to learn. There is hope for all who will sit at his feet! The Holy Spirit is the author of the most profound and scholarly Book ever written. The impress of his mastermind is in every page of the Bible. "The Spirit searcheth all things, yea, the deep things of God" (1 Cor. 2:10). To think on the mind of the Spirit is to exclaim, "O the depth of the riches both of the wisdom and the knowledge of God! how unsearchable are his judgments, and his ways past tracing out!" (Rom. 11:33).

As to the Spirit's powers of volition, the remaining and perhaps the most conspicuous attribute of personality, Jesus himself gives us the best illustration. "The wind bloweth where it will," he said to Nicodemus, "so is every one that is born of the Spirit" (John 3:8). In other words, the Spirit is as free as the wind. He is utterly sovereign. He no more regards the rituals and programs of men with all their niceties and distinctions than the summer breeze follows the streets and the highways of man's design. Let us beware of pink-tea patterns of worship. Usually they reflect man's schemes more than the Spirit's sovereignty. He refuses to be bound by precedent and in every new circumstance remains at liberty to work his own good pleasure.

Two other passages come to mind in this connection, pointing up the supremacy of the Spirit in the affairs of the church. In reviewing the impressive array of gifts bestowed upon the talented church at Corinth, Paul makes clear that in them all "worketh the one and the same Spirit, dividing to each one severally *even as he will*"

(1 Cor. 12:11). On the Isle of Patmos John heard our risen Lord, the glorified head of the church, place unmistakable emphasis upon the sovereignty of the Holy Spirit by his solemn and seven times repeated admonition: "He that hath an ear, let him hear *what the Spirit saith* to the churches" (Rev. 3:6).

If I seem to belabor the fact that the Spirit is a distinct person of the Godhead, it is because I have found that many Christians have encountered difficulties precisely at this point.

In the initial experience of salvation they have done business with the Saviour. Many times they have prayed to the Father and have received answers to their prayers. But the Holy Spirit, as a person, has never been real to them, nor can they speak of anything definite which has brought him into the orbit of their consciousness. The firsthandedness of such an experience can come only when they realize the Holy Spirit is a person, with all the glorious attributes of personality. The business they do with him must be as much on a person-to-person basis as that which they have transacted with the Father and with the Son.

In this connection, one word more needs to be said about the place within the Trinity generally assigned to the Holy Spirit. His position is one of equality with the Father and with the Son. By no means is he least because he is mentioned last. Lest this might seem the case, remember that he has been given the designation *Holy,* and blasphemy against him alone is unpardonable. As the Son was from the beginning co-existent with the Father, so it is with the "eternal Spirit" (Heb. 9:14). Ours is indeed a triune God and well may we say:

Glory be to the Father, and to the Son,
and to the Holy Ghost;
As it was in the beginning, is now,
and ever shall be, world without end, Amen.

H. W. GREATOREX

A DISTINCTION IN OFFICE

The same distinction in the persons of the Godhead will be found also in the office of each. Whereas the Father, Son, and Holy Spirit are active in every step of redemption, it is only natural that there should be a difference in the function of each. To recognize the difference in operation is to co-operate more intelligently in the fulfilment of God's purposes.

The late Dr. James McKee Adams, of the Southern Baptist Theological Seminary, Louisville, Kentucky, made a statement on this differential which has remained with me since my student days to bring enriching insight into the divine operation within the human heart. He said in effect, "God the Father is the *originating* cause; God the Son is the *mediating* cause; and God the Holy Spirit is the *effecting* cause." We shall see how Scripture and Christian experience repeat this diversity, setting forth at the same time the oneness of the Godhead and the distinction which always exists in the official work of each member of the Trinity.

For example, in the account of creation (Gen. 1:1) we read the sublimely simple statement: "In the beginning God created the heavens and the earth." This, I take it, describes the activity of the Father, the originating Cause. Turning to John 1:3 we read concerning the Word, "All things were made through him; and without him was not anything made that hath been made." The Son, therefore, was likewise active in creation, but as Mediator. In the clearer light of the New Testament the figure of Genesis 1:2 graphically describes the part which the third member of the Trinity had in creation: "And the Spirit of God was brooding upon the face of the waters" (see margin). In the beginning, as when a man becomes a new creature in Christ Jesus, the Spirit broods over the chaos wrought by sin to make effective the Word of God and to bring Light where there was darkness.

Let us take prayer as a representative experience in the realm of redemption. There, also, the Father, Son, and Spirit are active and always in the relation just described. Turn to Ephesians 2:18 and note how this distinction obtains. "For through him [Christ] we both [the Gentiles who were afar off, and the Jews who were nigh] have our access in one Spirit unto the Father." As is so often the case, the prepositions tell the story—"through," "in," and "unto." Prayer is addressed to God the Father, (the originating Cause) but our approach and his answer are always through the Son (the mediating Cause), and prayer, to be effectual, must know the quickening touch of the Spirit (the effecting Cause).

A striking symbol of the teamwork of the Trinity operative in redemption is afforded in the realm of medicine. There are three professions involved in the treatment of disease: the physician who diagnoses the case and prescribes the treatment; the pharmacist who compounds the remedy; and the nurse who faithfully waits at the patient's bedside and administers that which the doctor has prescribed and the druggist has prepared. In the analogy, of course, the physician represents the Father, who has diagnosed the need of the sinner and prescribed the remedy.

The druggist represents the Son, who by achieving a perfect human life provides through his shed blood the only specific cure for sin. The nurse represents the Holy Spirit, who applies the remedy by quickening the Word to challenge the faith of the sinner.[1] I like this analogy because it shows so strikingly the loving and practical nature of the Spirit's part in recovery from the disease of sin. Anyone who has been seriously sick knows what it means to have a faithful nurse constantly attending his bedside, administering every aid, and literally pulling him through his illness. The Holy Spirit is like that.

Speaking of our salvation, someone has well said: "The Father thought it, the Son brought it, and the Holy Spirit wrought it." This states the case and is the reason I have presented the Holy Spirit in this chapter as the Executor. He is the executive member of the Trinity; he has always been so and ever will be. This relation is an eternal one. God's message to Joshua and Zerubbabel is for all of us. "Not by might, nor by power, but *by my Spirit,* saith Jehovah of hosts" (Zech. 4:6). The man Christ Jesus acknowledged this when he explained to the Pharisees how he was getting his mighty works done. "I by the Spirit of God cast out demons" (Matt. 12:28). Even the offering of himself upon the cross as a sacrifice without blemish unto God was "through the eternal Spirit" (Heb. 9:14). When shall we recognize this Executive of the Godhead for what he is? How long will it take us to learn that whatever the task in the realm of redemption, he is the one who actually gets it done. He it is who convicts, who regenerates, who sanctifies us by weaving God's truth into the warp and

---

[1] I regret that I am unable to name the friend to whom I am indebted for this instructive parallel.

woof of our character. He came to do *in* us all that Christ came to do *for* us. This leads us to another distinction.

A DISTINCTION IN METHOD

We must also recognize that the Holy Spirit goes about his work in a manner distinct from Father and Son. There is a difference both in his mode of procedure and in the realm of his activity. He works within the heart of man. What he does, therefore, is inward, subjective. Jesus said in John 14:17, "He abideth with you, and shall be *in* you." We are slow to believe what God has said concerning the indwelling Spirit and to receive him consciously and deliberately as our Lord. Once we do receive him thus, however, our whole life is changed. His presence within makes the difference. How could it be otherwise?

Many passages of God's Word teach us that the Holy Spirit dwells within every regenerate heart. Paul asks the Corinthians, "Know ye not that your body is a temple of the Holy Spirit which is in you, which ye have from God?" (1 Cor. 6:19). He was thinking of a temple as God's dwelling place. In the light of Scripture one cannot deny this fact without accepting the alternative that he is not a Christian at all. "But ye are not in the flesh but in the Spirit, if so be that the Spirit of God dwelleth in you. But if any man hath not the Spirit of Christ, he is none of his. And if Christ is in you, the body is dead because of sin; but the spirit is life because of righteousness. But if the Spirit of him that raised up Jesus from the dead dwelleth in you, he that raised up Christ Jesus from the dead shall give life also to your mortal bodies through his Spirit that dwelleth in you" (Rom. 8:9–11).

This passage emphasizes two things: the fact of the

Spirit's indwelling and the purpose of that indwelling. Note the word "dwell." Literally, it means "make one's home in." Underscore the word in the preceding quotation. It occurs three times, making it unmistakably plain that the Spirit of God has come to make his home within you if you are a believer. He is not there as a visitor, as a transient guest who takes his leave when things go wrong. He is there as one who has come to stay. He has moved in to make himself at home.

We can more readily understand how necessarily subjective the Spirit's work is by comparing it to that of the Son. We can see the Lord Jesus struggling up the steep slope of Calvary with his cross to die thereon in full payment for our sin. What we cannot see so readily, however, is the Spirit striving up the steep slope of self-will within us, seeking to make that cross effective there in dealing with our own stubborn pride. And because we cannot see him, we fail sometimes to understand and take an intelligent part in the process.

The divine Executive has come to dwell within us. The purpose of his indwelling is to quicken, to cause us to participate in the very life of Jesus. That is, of course, the whole purpose of salvation, and the Holy Spirit has come to see that this purpose is realized by each one who believes. I repeat, he has come to do *in* us all that our Saviour came to do *for* us. If Christ made salvation available, the Holy Spirit makes it effective. After he has done his work he carries it on out to others. Of course, the two processes really go on at the same time, but he cannot do much through us until first he has wrought freely in us.

A veteran of the cross once remarked to me, "I have learned to count on the silent, unseen work of the Holy

Spirit." We may not always be aware of the process, but while we are looking unto Jesus who is the author and finisher of our faith, the Holy Spirit is busy revealing him not only to us but through us to others. We cannot see the Spirit at work but we can count on him and give him the willing co-operation of an intelligent faith. Only thus can he work at his best.

Let me sum up what I have tried to say concerning the divine Executor by telling you about the first money I ever inherited, a fifty-dollar Liberty Bond which was sent to me while I was a student in the seminary. This was willed to me by an aunt. Many years later I was holding a series of meetings in Clinton, North Carolina, county seat of Samson County, where my aunt had lived and died. At the time I was doing much thinking and praying on the theme of this chapter. After services one day, a lawyer introduced himself to me and asked if I remembered him. I was forced to confess that I did not recall having met him before. Then, by way of identifying himself, he asked, "Do you remember getting a fifty-dollar Liberty Bond from your Aunt Molly's estate?" "Yes," I replied—who could forget such an amount in student days! "Well," he continued, "I was the executor of her will. I am the one who sent you that bond."

I thanked him again for his kindness, and so far as he knew that closed the incident. But he had started me to thinking. As soon as I got home I asked a lawyer to tell me what an executor was and to explain the difference between an executor and an administrator. He told me that an administrator was someone appointed by the court to carry out the provisions of a will, whereas the executor was one named in the will itself to do so. And then I asked another question. "If some money has been willed to me, is there any way I can get it except through the executor or administrator of that will?" He replied, "There is no other legal way you could come into possession of your inheritance."

I had my answer. The New Testament is God's will. That is exactly what the word "testament" means—God's last will and testament. In it he has bequeathed all his vast wealth to his heirs. But there is this about a will: it cannot go into effect until the death of the one who made it. "For where a testament is, there must of necessity be the death of him that made it" (Heb. 9:16). Now, God the Father could not die; but God the Son could, and did. It was his death on the cross that put this New Testament into effect. We can see now the deeper meaning in our Lord's words when, instituting the Lord's Supper, he said: "This cup is the new covenant [testament] in my blood" (Luke 22:20). And this will or testament specifically names the Holy Spirit as the Executor, the one and the only one who sees to it that its rich provisions are carried into effect whenever its terms are met.

That you may know this Executor, this other Comforter, better and through his wonderful ministry enter more fully into the rich provisions of the Father's love is the purpose of this book.

II

Dealing with
Our Foremost Problem

Some years ago the Baptist pastors of North Carolina were gathered in a session at our church in their annual meeting prior to the state convention. They had arranged an attractive program. The topic of discussion on this particular occasion was "A Pastor's Problems." One of the men in the opening words of his fine address said, "The greatest problem any pastor has on any field and in any situation is *himself*." The experience of every man present whispered deep within, "Amen." He was right. In every department of his work—visiting the sick, counseling with the perplexed, praying, or preaching—a pastor's greatest problem is himself. It is nothing short of appalling that a preacher may deliver a thoroughly orthodox sermon and yet preach not Christ but himself.

But this difficulty is in no way confined to pastors alone. Every man's chief problem is himself. The more noble his endeavor, the more distressing are the intrusions of self-interest whenever they appear. Whatever the avenue of service may be, the occasion is marred and the fruit blighted when self comes into view. And come into view it will, if it is there at all. People are quick to sense its presence and to stumble over it, even in its most subtle forms. Few, indeed, have the grace to receive the good and overlook the stumbling block of self-interest. And of this we may be sure—if self is offensive to our fellow man, it is infinitely more so to God.

Now, theoretically, at least, one can easily see how God has disposed of this problem in the life of the believer. He has made his procedure very plain. He has gone so far as to dramatize it vividly in the act of baptism which stands at the beginning of the Christian life. In this beautiful symbolism the believer affirms his part in Christ's death upon the cross. In accepting Christ, he has accepted Christ's death as well. Thus he may exclaim with Paul, "I have been crucified with Christ" (Gal. 2:20). Having been crucified with him, it is only natural and reasonable to be buried with him also. After death comes burial. Hence, in God's sight the rebel self, the "big I," the apartness-from-God which is the essence of sin, is dead and buried—"forgotten as a dead man out of mind" (Psalm 31:12).

The rest of the picture is equally clear. For "if we died with Christ, we believe that we shall also live with him" (Rom. 6:8). The believer's part in the resurrection of Jesus is as real and effective as it is in his death. Resurrection life—God's sort of life—is imparted to him through faith in Jesus. In Christ he has now become a new creature—all things have become new (2 Cor. 5:17). Thus, the remaining step in the act of baptism is fraught with a meaning of equal importance. By faith the true Christian has participated in both the death and resurrection of Christ. The picture is dramatically accurate. "We were buried therefore with him through baptism into death: that like as Christ was raised from the dead through the glory of the Father, so we also might walk in newness of life" (Rom. 6:4).

It is not in theory but in practice that the difficulty comes. The young believer does not journey far before he discovers through painful experience that if self is dead, it is the *livest* dead thing he has ever encountered. On every hand, in ways as subtle as strong, self bobs up. It intrudes upon one's holiest moments, nor is its hideous nature refined one whit by the passing of time. If anything, it seems increasingly ugly and repulsive. Romans 7 tells the story of this struggle. The Christian's own experience echoes the cry of Paul, "O wretched man that I am! who shall deliver me from the body of this death?" (Rom. 7:24, KJV).

The picture so clearly presented in baptism has become distorted. The theory has not stood the test of experience —or, at least, so it seems. As a consequence, far too many Christians, confused and discouraged, abandon the whole idea as a hopeless paradox and accept as inevitable the wretchedness of a life constantly torn between the contending forces of flesh and spirit. But others are convinced that the gospel supplies something better than defeat and contradiction. For them the struggle continues until, brought face to face with their own utter helplessness, they find the victory which God provides through the Spirit of Christ living within them.

To make this victory ours is the first work of the Holy Spirit after that of regeneration. It is his great emphasis in Romans 6, 7, and 8. This aspect of his ministry is strikingly set forth in Romans 8:13, "But if by the Spirit ye put to death the deeds of the body, ye shall live." If we study these words carefully, they will tell us how the Holy Spirit solves our foremost problem.

WHAT IS TO BE PUT TO DEATH?

Death is sometimes a terrible, ghastly affair. Always it is a solemn experience, and God never refers to it lightly. We will, therefore, do well to ponder the question, What is it about us that must die?

The plain answer from Scripture is "the deeds of the body." Not the *body* but the *deeds* of the body. And right here let me make it very plain that God has no quarrel against the physical organism we call our body. There is nothing that smacks of asceticism or of that "show of wisdom in will-worship and humility and *severity to the body*" which is evident in some circles, but which is "not of any value against the indulgence of the flesh" (Col. 2:23). God speaks of the body in terms of the highest respect and wants us to regard it as sacred, the temple of his own Holy Spirit. We shall have to look for the meaning beyond flesh and blood or the perfectly normal appetites of the body.

The reference is clearly to something else, and the word "deeds" gives us the clue. It is the same word as that found in the title of the fifth book of the New Testament, "The *Acts* of the Apostles." God pronounces this sentence of condemnation upon the "doings" (margin of ASV), the practices of a body which he described in Romans 6:8 as "the body of sin." The motions of that body—sin incorporated—work through the old selfish and fallen nature that is still with us. The same idea is advanced in Colossians 3:5-9: "Put to death therefore your members which are upon the earth: fornication, uncleanness, passion, evil desire, and covetousness . . . put them all away: anger, wrath, malice, railing, shameful speaking out of your mouth: lie not one to another; seeing you have put off the old man with his *doings*." The culprit is thus easily identified.

From God's viewpoint, which is that of eternity, the "old man" has been dealt with once and for all—crucified with Christ; from our viewpoint, here in time and place, this death by crucifixion must be *applied* to his "doings" in a day by day process. It is at this point that the Holy Spirit stands ready to render invaluable aid.

But before passing on to see how this aid is given, let us be honest with ourselves in answering one question: Are we really convinced that the culprit we have identified as our "old man" deserves such severe treatment? Are we ready to agree with God's findings when he says that all we are or can become through our natural heritage is so depraved by reason of sin that its every expression in thought and impulse merits only the answer of death? There are many who do not think so. Instead, their sympathies actually go out to the offender when the death-dealing process is about to go into effect.

We are in this respect like the world which, forgetting the shocking nature of the crime and the requirements of justice, feels only compassion for the criminal when he finally pays the debt in death to the society that he has wronged. For this reason newspapers which carry the vivid account of an execution usually present at the same time a review of the offense for which the penalty was exacted.

This is an effort of the press to strike a balance between crime and its penalty, and I think well of it. It would be a good thing for us as Christians to do likewise. When we are tempted to self-pity, let us turn to God's Word and review the nature both of the offense and of the offender.

Many times when the Holy Spirit, through some incident—usually painful and humiliating—applies the shame of the cross to this monstrous thing in our lives, we fail to remember its perverse and sinful nature. We even seek to avert the execution of the death sentence upon the very thing that hurts us. If we are honest with ourselves, however, we must realize that we are not yet willing to yield up all to the death of the cross. Like Saul of old we want to save back the best—the more refined and cultured expressions of self—for a sacrifice to God. God's answer to this defiance of his judgment is as pertinent today as then: "Behold, to obey is better than sacrifice, and to hearken than the fat of rams" (1 Sam. 15:22). A broken and contrite heart is the only sacrifice acceptable to God, and the only way the stubborn heart of self can be broken is to see itself as God sees it.

Let us, then, examine the case God has made out against self or that which Paul so often describes as the "flesh"— for I believe the two terms are virtually synonymous. It would seem that when Paul speaks of the flesh he is usually referring to that which we call "self" in its hateful sense. Just how comprehensive this term is one may gather from the words of Jesus who said to Nicodemus, "That which is born of the flesh is flesh" (John 3:6). This definition includes a vast realm. It describes all that we are by virtue of our first birth and is in direct contrast to the term "spirit," which describes all that we become by virtue of our second birth. We must observe the distinction which Jesus made: "That which is born of the flesh is flesh; that which is born of the spirit is spirit."

The Word of God brings a fearful exposé of corruption hidden in this fallen nature. Discussing with the Pharisees the distinction between ceremonial and real defilement, Jesus gave an X-ray picture of the human heart. "For from within, out of the heart of men, evil thoughts proceed, fornications, thefts, murders, adulteries, covetings, wickedness, deceit, lasciviousness, an evil eye, railing, pride, foolishness; *all these evil things proceed from within,* and defile the man" (Mark 7:21–23).

Paul paints a similar picture in Galatians 5:19–21: "Now the works of the flesh are manifest, which are these: fornication, uncleanness, lasciviousness, idolatry, sorcery, enmities, strife, jealousies, wraths, factions, divisions, parties, envyings, drunkenness, revellings, and such like: of which I forewarn you, even as I did forewarn you, that they who practise such things shall not inherit the kingdom of God." There can be no mistake about it. According to the Scriptures, the guilt of the offender is clearly established.

Perhaps this is not the time in our discussion to argue the case, but someone may say, "I am not guilty of such as that." Wait a moment! In the light of the Sermon on the Mount, every hateful, unloving thought is the seed of murder. Every selfish motive is the seed of jealousy, covetousness, and idolatry. Every self-indulgence carries the germ of drunkenness and addictions. Can we still say we are not guilty? In the light of God's holiness we must admit that the potential of every one of these sins is hidden deep in the inner recesses of our nature.

But we must follow God's indictment of the flesh one

step more. "The mind of the flesh is enmity against God; for it is not subject to the law of God, neither indeed *can* it be" (Rom. 8:7). The case is hopeless. The criminal is incorrigible. It is a painful revelation that after years of Christian living, the thoughts, the motives, and all the "doings" that stem from this old nature are as vile and black as at the beginning. God attempts no improvement for there can be none. The death sentence is the only answer he can give to its incurable enmity. The flesh is neither the author nor the agent of any good thing, and God rules it out. The more carefully we take the case under review, the more heartily must we concur in the just sentence of death which God has imposed on this sinful self, and the more gratefully and intelligently shall we seek to work with him for its execution.

HOW IS IT TO BE PUT TO DEATH?

Having established the identity of the offender, and having become convinced both as to his guilt and the justice of his sentence, our next question is, How is this decree of death to be made effective in daily experience? How is the self-life which meets us at every turn to be put out of the way?

Certainly not by the energy of the flesh. If self puts out self, what but self can remain? I once heard a young Christian who had been wrestling with this problem pray, "Lord, help me to crucify myself." He was painfully aware of his difficulty. There could be no question about that which he desired, but his prayer indicated he did not know *how* God goes about this matter. No man can crucify himself. It is a physical impossibility. One may commit suicide in many different ways, but if he ever dies by crucifixion, someone else will put him on the cross. That is also true spiritually.

The Holy Spirit is the agent who brings this to pass. As the verse before us specifically states, "If ye *by the Spirit* do put to death the deeds of the body, ye shall live" (Rom. 8:13). However, in order to understand how the Spirit works with us to put the death sentence into effect, we must give some thought to the Greek word translated "put to death." The verb is built on the stem *thanatos,* which, as you who are familiar with William Cullen Bryant's famous poem "Thanatopsis" will recognize, is the Greek word for death. To this substantive has been added a causative ending. Actually, therefore, the idea of the verb is *"cause* to be put to death." In fact, it is so translated in Mark 13:12: "and children shall rise up against their parents, and shall *cause them to be put to death"* (KJV). Even in the fierce persecutions which were predicted in this passage, the children would not themselves be the actual slayers of their parents. By taking some attitude or by speaking some word they would cause others to do the murder.

Note also in Mark 14:55 where the word occurs again: "And the chief priests and all the council sought for witness against Jesus *to put him to death;* and found none" (KJV). It was probably true that the hatred of the chief priests against Jesus was so great that they would have done away with him themselves, but if I understand them, they did not care to soil their hands with the bloody business if they could get others to do it for them. Their only desire was to *get it done.* Now, accepting this meaning of the word, our problem is greatly simplified. We are not to crucify ourselves; we are only to say the word that will be the occasion for another to get it done.

That other one, of course, is the Holy Spirit of God who carries into effect the death penalty imposed on the rebel self. Our position is that of a judge who pronounces the sentence but who leaves the execution of it to another. In the case of the old self-life, the Holy Spirit is the one divinely appointed to this work. In our previous chapter we saw him as the divine Executor. Here he is the divine Executioner. But he must have our permission. We must say the word, because God does nothing in us without our own active co-operation.

An experience some years ago brought home to me this aspect of the Holy Spirit's ministry. We had at that time a pet dog named Skipper which had won his way into our affections—especially those of our children. One day Skipper was struck by a passing automobile. Though he recovered in a measure from his injury, Skipper was never himself again. His disposition was ruined and he became a problem in the neighborhood. One day after he had snapped at my little daughter I sent him to the veterinarian for observation. The doctor explained that sometimes a dog's disposition was permanently altered by an injury of that nature. He stated that Skipper would probably be a dangerous pet to have with little children in the home and frankly advised me to put him out of the way.

The veterinarian had made his recommendation. He stood ready to carry out the course that he had advised. But the problem was mine—the dog was mine, and the children were mine. It was my responsibility to say the word, and I said it. I have always felt that I said the right word, and ever since I have held in grateful appreciation the friend who counseled me so wisely and who then so faithfully did the "dirty work" for me. So far as I know that is the only sentence of execution I have pronounced—except that which time and time again I pronounce when the Holy Spirit reveals to me the working of a vicious nature within and waits my word to carry out the death sentence which he so strongly recommends.

My relation to Skipper in the incident referred to above designates the position which the believer must take in regard to the problem of self. But the act of pronouncing God's sentence must be cultivated until it becomes a habit of mind. That attitude is described in Romans 6:11 where Paul says, "Even so *reckon* ye also yourselves to be dead unto sin, but alive unto God in Christ Jesus." The tense of the verb is present, indicating a continuing process of reckoning. The figure is that of a bookkeeper making his entries, or of a navigator setting his course in a given direction. Appearances to the contrary, our old man has been crucified, as God's Word plainly states. "Ye died, and your life is hid with Christ in God" (Col. 3:3). "They that are of Christ Jesus have crucified the flesh with the passions and the lusts thereof" (Gal. 5:24). The inference is unavoidable. The thing is done. The crucifixion has already taken place. By faith we must accept the bearings God has given us and hold to the course in a steady reckoning.

The idea involved in this faith-reckoning is well illustrated by an expression with which all who enjoy the old-fashioned game of croquet are familiar. One player by hitting another's ball obtains two strokes, but he cannot repeat the play unless he makes his wicket. Somehow it always gave me a lot of satisfaction to make that particular shot. Leaving my opponent in as disadvantageous a position as possible, I would shoot for position and then attempt to go through my wicket. As often as not, however,

I would fail in my second try, and thus the play would pass to others. Sometimes, on my next turn, forgetful of the rules in my eagerness to gain a stroke, I would get set to hit his ball again. But my opponent stopping me would protest, "Hold on there. You can't make that play. Don't you remember? You have not made your wicket. You're *dead on me.*" And so I was. I could not deny the desire to make the play, but according to the rules of the game I was "dead" in relation to his ball until I had gone through the wicket.

According to God's Book we are "dead" to the whole triumvirate of evil—the world, the flesh, and the devil. In times of temptation we cannot honestly say the appeal is not there. It *is* there, and often very powerfully there. Allowed to stage its setting, the devil can make any sin attractive. This business of being "dead" to sin does not necessarily take away its appeal, nor does it render us incapable of responding. We are free to do as we choose. God's will is that we play by the rules he has given—quietly reckoning ourselves dead unto sin and alive unto God just as he has said. And the wonderful thing about it is that the instant we make this reckoning and take the position that he has indicated in reference to sin, the whole problem is solved and the victory is won. It is a sure way, and the only way by which the believer may walk in constant victory.

THE REWARD OF SO DOING

Thus far we have been thinking of God's solution to this problem in negative terms. We have dwelt at some length on guilt and its penalty, so much so that we may be in danger of overlooking the positive emphasis in the divine procedure. According to God's plan, the death we have been discussing is not an end in itself but the means to an end. That end is our experience of God's kind of life in an ever-increasing degree of fullness. It is a death-life process which the Spirit is working out in us, a process in which death is incidental to the life which he can give only to those who receive it from this approach.

Eternal life—God's kind of life—is available to us through his Son Jesus Christ, and through him alone. That is generally understood. "And the witness is this, that God gave unto us eternal life, and this life is in his Son" (1 John 5:11). What is not so generally understood, however, is that the life which Jesus gives is resurrection life, and only that which has died can experience it. The hand that reaches out to take it must bear the print of the nails. Thus, in the kingdom of God, we die in order to live, and the degree to which we become conformed to Christ's death determines the degree to which we experience the power of his resurrection (Phil. 3:10).

In one respect, of course, Christ's death was unique, "Christ died for our sins" (1 Cor. 15:3). He endured what we deserve. The full penalty of sin he took upon himself. While we may not fathom the mystery in his cry of desolation, we may safely gather from it that there on the cross he absorbed in his own body the shame and suffering which sin always incurs as its inevitable penalty. In this aspect of Christ's death the believer does not enter; indeed, he cannot do so for the simple reason that Christ endured it for him.

But there is another aspect of Christ's death into which the believer does enter. "For the death he died, he died unto sin once for all" (Rom. 6:10, margin). The preposition *unto* (in respect to) tells the story. In this death *to* sin every believer has a part. Christ loved us enough to endure the awful penalty of sin for us. He loved us more, even, than that. He loved us enough to *pass the effect of his death on to us.* That death, now robbed of its sting, occurs in the believer the moment he puts his trust in Jesus. So painlessly and instantly does it take effect that he often is unaware of what has happened until in the light of God's Word he sees the deed as done and makes his adjustment accordingly.

Failure to grasp the positive emphasis in this death-life principle has resulted in untold harm. It has obscured the meaning of the cross in the experiences of the Christian —both to himself and to others. It has made the cross an end instead of a means, a denial instead of an affirmation, a symbol of repression instead of release.

In his classic reference to the grain of wheat, our Lord illustrates the positive nature of this process. "Verily, verily, I say unto you, except a grain of wheat fall into the earth and die, it abideth alone; but if it die, it beareth much fruit" (John 17:24). Conceivably there are conditions in which a grain of wheat might fall into the earth and die (perish) without bearing fruit, just as there are certain "self-denials" and other morbid forms of repression which are not fruitful in the human personality. According to the divine plan, however, both in nature and redemption, the principle we are discussing is altogether wholesome and creative. Self-denial from God's point of view becomes self-realization.

In the process of "dying," the grain of wheat yields itself to nourish the germ of life within it. The soil that hides this mystery, the seasons of sunshine and rain which evoke it, are all conditions necessary and conducive to nature's process of self-realization. Only under such circumstances can the nourishing elements of the grain become available to the germ of life, and only under such circumstances can the germ of life appropriate the nourishment provided for its fulfilment in fruit a hundredfold.

In 2 Corinthians 4:7–15 the great apostle Paul illustrates the way in which the Holy Spirit transfers this principle into the realm of human endeavor and applies it to the circumstances around us. In a series of verbs packed with emotion and carefully balanced one against the other, Paul speaks of the trials and triumphs of the Christian ministry. "Pressed on every side, yet not straitened; perplexed, yet not unto despair; pursued, yet not forsaken; smitten down, yet not destroyed; always bearing about in the body the dying of Jesus, that the life also of Jesus may be manifested in our body." Then he concludes: "So then *death worketh in us* but *life* in you." In effect he says that he has been buried under successive avalanches of adversity, but it has been in all a fruitful experience. The circumstances in which he bore in his body "the dying of Jesus" proved the very circumstances in which also "the life of Jesus" became manifested in his body, and it is that manifestation that counts for himself and for others.

Adversity—the earth closing in about us—in whatever form it may come serves this useful purpose: it articulates our own self-will. What we want becomes all the more pronounced by reason of our frustration. The Holy Spirit sees to it that along with adversity the light and warmth of God's love is at work to make the experience a season of fruitfulness. Against the background of what we want, we can now see more clearly what God wants, and when once the two alternatives are clearly understood, the choice between them is simple enough. To deny the self that is outside of the will of God becomes simply a preliminary step to affirming the self that lies within that will. Thus by reason of the cross, the fertile soil of adversity yields an abundant harvest, and the burial ground of shattered hopes but sets the stage for the re-enactment of resurrection victory.

In the cross of Christ, therefore, we see the kind of death that brings life to ourselves and to others. For the Christian, the experience of that cross is at once an act and an attitude, a crisis which unfolds in a process. The death which begins to take effect when the believer first accepts Christ must be wrought by daily experience through his entire being until every vestige of the old self-will has felt its effect. Trials and adversities serve the advantage of exposing that self-will so that he can turn it over to the Spirit of God and let him deal with it through the cross.

In the treatment of a disease the physician must first isolate the germ. Then he must find a way of dealing death to that germ without at the same time injuring the patient. God faces the same kind of problem in dealing death to the sin that still lingers with us. He must destroy it without at the same time destroying the nerve of our own initiative. The cross stands ready for this business, but before it becomes effective in us, we must choose to have it so. When we make that choice the quickening process is bound to follow.

When Paul gave this promise of which we have been thinking (Rom. 8:13), it is likely that he had in mind life's fullness rather than its fruitfulness. The two ideas of degree and effectiveness, of course, belong together. But I feel that many Christians have failed to appreciate the element of degree. They seem to regard eternal life as something static. They are too easily content with having it and not eager enough to live it. Jesus came not only that we might have life but that we might enjoy it to an ever-abounding degree. No follower of his should be content to stop with anything less.

This difference of degree becomes immediately apparent when we consider an individual in different stages of growth. A week-old baby lies in his little crib. Tiptoe quietly to his side and look. He sleeps there with the face of a cherub. He is alive all right and radiant with health, but he spends most of his time sleeping. A few hours during the twenty-four he is awake to nurse at his mother's breast and to gaze with wondering eyes at this bright new world into which he is born. Then, contented, he falls again into dreamless sleep.

The infant son is alive all right and perfectly normal. But to what *degree* is he alive? Let the years pass, twenty of them, twenty-three, twenty-four of them. Look at him now—still a picture of health, clean in life and limb. His body has matured to the strength of manhood; his well-disciplined mind is stored with the treasure of the ages; his spirit rejoices in the fellowship of God to whom he has yielded his life in happy service. In body, mind, and spirit, he thrills in response to the challenge of all that life offers. Both are alive, the babe and the man, yet how vastly more so is the man than the babe. Even so, eternal life is a matter of degree. God having imparted his life to us is ceaselessly striving to bring us into maturity till we all attain unto a "full grown man, unto the measure of the stature of the fulness of Christ" (Eph. 4:13).

In this ceaseless struggle toward maturity the Holy Spirit has his appointed part. His great work is to quicken. However he may be associated with the death process, the association is for the one purpose of imparting life and yet more life. It was he who brought the still body of Jesus into glorious resurrection victory. And—never ceasing wonder of grace!—it is he who has come to make his home within our mortal bodies (Rom. 8:10–11). Things come alive at his touch. Life springs with the flow of his energy. We may unhesitatingly commit the problem of self to him in the quiet assurance that every ministry, whether that of song or testimony, prayer or preaching, will become vibrant with life—increasingly joyous, increasingly fruitful through the Spirit's cleansing power.

III

Kindling the
Fires of Devotion

The observant reader will find the imagery of the New Testament indescribably beautiful and expressive. Consider, for example, the figure presented in the words of Paul to his young friend Timothy: "For which cause I put thee in remembrance that thou stir up the gift of God, which is in thee through the laying on of hands" (2 Tim. 1:6). A more vivid translation is provided in the margin which would make it read, "Stir into flame the gift of God which is in thee." This phrase paints with glowing colors the picture of an open fire on a cold and cheerless day, friends gathered about, their faces reflecting its radiance, their hearts warmed by its cheer. As upon the hearth, however, so within the heart of man the flame of devotion sometimes flickers low. Our love for Christ burns out to cold gray ashes. At such a time the coals must be drawn together, fresh fuel must be added, and the smoldering embers fanned again into flame. It is my purpose in this chapter to show that the Holy Spirit, who is the very breath of God, will do this very thing if we permit him. His ministry is to tend the fires of devotion and keep them burning upon the altar within.

The right sort of devotional life is tremendously important. There can be no substitute for it. Whatever the nature of our own service, whether in the home or in the office or upon the farm, it is effective in the kingdom of God only as our love for Christ has been disciplined through hours of fellowship with him. In these busy times most of us have substituted working for the Lord for waiting on the Lord, doing for devotion, activity for adoration —and God is not pleased with the exchange.

In the controversy of the Bethany home, for example, we still sympathize with Martha more than Mary, even though Jesus clearly stated that Mary had chosen the better part. We feel this way because we are like Martha. We would rather serve Christ our way than his, which can only mean that we love ourselves more than we love him, and we might as well admit it. Cumbered with our much serving, we are not willing to enter into the secret of his presence and wait upon our Lord. The whole cause of Christ suffers from nothing more than it does from this lack of devotion on the part of those who profess to serve him.

Those who are truly great in Christian service have invariably drawn upon the unfailing resources of a rich devotional life. This is true of the saints of all ages. The apostle Paul is a striking example. A study of his epistles and the book of Acts with this in mind reveals the tremendous emphasis he placed upon communion with God. Back of all his ceaseless activity and explaining its fruitfulness was an uninterrupted prayer life. His writings are saturated with the Old Testament. The light that came from his pen was that of divine illumination, insights flashed upon his spirit in seasons of sacred intimacy with God. His habits of devotion are reflected even in the harsh routine of prison. One may gather from his instructions to Timothy that the study of Scripture had a part in his daily routine even there. "Bring . . . the books . . . especially the parchments" (2 Tim. 4:13). And in an earlier imprisonment, when he was in all probability chained to a soldier, Paul still maintained his habit of prayer. "For this cause I *bow my knees* unto the Father," he wrote to the Ephesians (3:14).

Even more impressive is the devotional life of Jesus. The late Dr. John R. Sampey said of him, "He dressed daily in the mirror of the Old Testament Scriptures." He lived on the Word of God, and his triumphal march across the pages of the Gospels is marked by the campfires of prayer and intercession. His teachings lay great stress upon the cultivation of the heart. When he said, "but give for alms those things which are within" (Luke 11:41), did he not mean that after all, a man's richest contribution to the world would be a noble heart-life? Certainly in these days when men's hearts are failing them, the world needs nothing more desperately than it needs men of strong inner life.

Breakdowns—physical, emotional, and moral—are due to this cause more than to any other. Our great weakness is at this point, and the reason for it lies in our failure to avail ourselves of God's proffered help. His desire is that we be "strengthened with power *through his Spirit* in the inward man" (Eph. 3:16). That inner strength is imparted in no other way.

Now, like breathing, the secret of maintaining a healthy

devotional life is a matter of twin action: prayer and Bible study. It would be as useless to argue which of the two is the more important as to argue which is more important in the process of breathing, inhaling or exhaling. Neither means anything without the other. I say this because I think there are more people who "say their prayers" with some degree of regularity than there are those who read their Bibles. But prayer under such circumstances withers and soon fades into the dry formality of vain repetition. Communion with God is necessarily a two-way avenue. In developing a vigorous inner life, prayer and Bible study go hand in hand by divine appointment. By divine appointment also is the ministry of the Holy Spirit, whose help in both these essentials no Christian can afford to ignore.

IN PRAYER

"And in like manner the Spirit also *helpeth* our infirmity: for we know not how to pray as we ought" (Rom. 8:26). I find no fault with the translation. *Help* is a good English word with honorable Anglo-Saxon origin, and here its meaning is perfectly plain. But the Greek word which it translates is a compound of three words requiring seventeen letters of the alphabet for its formation—*sun-anti-lambanetai*. Now, in all fairness, I submit that you cannot pour the combined effect of these three words of seventeen letters into one word of seven letters without losing something in the overflow! I would not have you suffer that loss, for the meaning is priceless.

The three words in the Greek are two prepositions and a verb. *Sun* is the preposition "with," *anti* is the preposition which means "at the other end of," and *lambanetai* is a verb which means to "take hold of." The late Dr. A. T. Robertson used to illustrate the idea in the preposition *anti* by the old fashioned game of "anti-over." He told his classes in Greek how, when he was a lad, boys and girls at school during recess would take their places on opposite sides of the schoolhouse and throw a ball over it to be caught by the other team. As he threw the ball, each player would shout, "Anti-over." This simple game admirably illustrates the root idea of the Greek preposition and the persistent way in which it has survived through the centuries. The picture, therefore, in this word translated "helpeth" is of one standing opposite another taking hold with him to lift a load too heavy for him to bear alone.

In my early teens I spent my summers on an uncle's farm in eastern North Carolina. There is a pungent colloquialism which he would use when he needed help in lifting or moving a heavy object. "Grab a holt, son," he would say, "and help me." I like that. It is just what the Holy Spirit offers to do for us with our burden of prayer. He will "grab a holt" with us to bring our prayer to God. We may be sure also that he will be carrying the heavy end of the burden as we make our way to the throne of grace.

"The Spirit also helpeth our infirmity." I call your attention to the fact that it is "infirmity," not "infirmities," as we might expect. The use of the singular indicates that in God's sight our one great weakness is in prayer. Of course, there are weaknesses all along the line with which the Spirit helps, but this is the parent weakness of them all. Out of prevailing prayer all other weaknesses may be overcome.

As with the disciples who could not cast the demon out of the epileptic boy (Mark 9:28–29), failure in prayer is our one great embarrassment. Man does not naturally pray. Please do not misunderstand me. It is quite natural for men to call for help when they are in deep distress. The heathen shipmates of Jonah, when the storm was great, "cried every man unto his god" (Jonah 1:5). But man does not naturally seek after God with that kind of seeking which is the essence of prayer (Rom. 3:11). The unregenerate man seeks his own welfare, not God's. "It is not a part of the natural life of man to pray. By 'natural' I mean the ordinary, sensible, healthy, worldly-minded life. . . . Prayer is an interruption to personal ambition, and no man who is busy has time to pray." [1] Prayer cuts across the grain of our natural inclinations, and the prayer habit is doomed to failure if undertaken in the energy of the flesh.

Taking all this into account, we ought not to be surprised when we come to the prayer period cold and indifferent, a great deal more interested in the thronging calls of the day than in God's call to intercession. Actually, this is quite normal. It would be surprising if it were otherwise. What else could one expect from a situation so adverse to prayer? Instead of quarreling with our inherent infirmity, therefore, let us recognize it and avail ourselves of the ever-present help proffered by the Holy Spirit.

We are in this respect somewhat like the receiving set of a radio. When we turn the switch, we are not surprised that music does not flow forth immediately, even when tuned to the right frequency. We wait to give the electric current time to flow through the tubes and make them warm and receptive. Just as without the current there can

[1] Oswald Chambers, *If Ye Shall Ask* (New York: Dodd, Mead & Co., 1938), p. 2.

be no response in the receiving set, so without the vital
presence of the Holy Spirit there can be no response in our
hearts for prayer.

I have found it thus, and I challenge you, next time you
undertake to pray, to make the experiment for yourself.
By some conscious expression of faith confess the embarrassment of your own prayerlessness and recognize the
presence of your Helper. Put your hand in his and quietly
commit the season of prayer to him without worrying too
much about your coldness and indifference. He will understand, and before long you will find him faithfully taking
hold with you to make the hour indescribably sweet. The
author of that lovely hymn, "Sweet Hour of Prayer,"
must have been thinking of this when he spoke of "Him
whose truth and faithfulness engage the waiting soul to
bless."

The remainder of this illuminating passage of Scripture
describes two outstanding features of the Spirit's ministry
in prayer. "For we know not how to pray as we ought; but
the Spirit himself maketh intercession [falls in with us]
for us with *groanings which cannot be uttered;* and he that
searcheth the hearts knoweth what is the mind of the
Spirit, because he maketh intercession for the saints *according to the will of God.*" Prayer quickened by the Spirit
is marked by its *earnestness* and its *concern only for the
will of God.*

Until the Spirit of God comes upon us with unutterable
longings, our prayers are cold and indifferent, their vigor
dissipated by many distractions. The earnestness which
gives them point and meaning is not a product of our
effort but of his. It is possible to work up a lather of emotion, like the frenzy of the prophets of Baal (1 Kings

18:26–28) before the altar on Mount Carmel, and to delude ourselves into thinking that we shall be heard for our much speaking. The "groanings which cannot be uttered," however, are not self-induced. They are the work of the Holy Spirit who moves upon us to make our prayer effectual, and effectual prayer rests upon Christ's agony, not ours.

What the Spirit does is to gather all our longings and bring them into the sharp focus of one intense desire, just as the lens of a magnifying glass gathers the rays of the sun into one spot of burning heat. At such a time the child of God becomes wonderingly aware that his prayer has far greater meaning than he himself is able to realize, and his own desires are freighted with a longing altogether inexpressible.

The second mark of the Spirit's ministry in prayer is a concern only for the will of God to be done. It is quite natural for us to interpret difficulties in terms of our own advantage or disadvantage and then to seek the solution that seems best to us. That is exactly the trouble with so much that we call prayer; it is self-centered. "Ye ask, and receive not, because ye ask amiss, that ye may spend it in your pleasures" (James 4:3). Praying never gets beyond this stage until the Spirit of God takes over.

But how can one's asking be otherwise than prompted by self-interest? If a man is to be sincere, must he not ask for that which he wants, whatever his wants may be? By all means. Our greatest asset in any prayer experience is our *wanting*. Trouble makes a rich contribution to prayer because it accentuates this sense of need. Need begets desire, and desire is the only vehicle on which the burden of prayer may be loaded. The Holy Spirit, recognizing this, takes our sense of need and, by a true interpretation of our circumstances in the light of the cross, transmutes it to become the desire to see God's will done and not ours.

I say "true interpretation," for our own interpretation is distorted by self-interest. But once we have seen the good thing that God has hidden away in a set of circumstances and recognize that it so far surpasses anything that we have possibly imagined, we want it—*his* way and *not ours*. Thus, the vehicle of our desire becomes freighted with God's longings, and with great liberty we plead the name of Jesus. Thenceforth, our assurance is that "if we ask anything according to his will, he heareth us: and if we know that he heareth us whatsoever we ask, we know that we have the petitions which we have asked of him" (1 John 5:14–15). Our Father who "searcheth the hearts" is looking to see if we have found the "mind of the Spirit" or his construction of our circumstances. Once that has been found, the answer to our prayer is gloriously certain. This ministry of the Spirit is the secret of prevailing prayer.

With such an approach, prayer can never drop into a dull and monotonous routine. The child of God finds himself surrounded with a continually changing and challenging set of circumstances. Life becomes kaleidoscopic. The basic elements may remain the same, but the pattern about which they are to be arranged in the will of God is different each day and always indescribably beautiful.

The realization of this truth has come to me lately with blessed release. If I may put it personally, there are two who intercede for me. One, my advocate Jesus Christ the righteous, is at the right hand of the Majesty on high bearing in his scars the very marks of my redemption which are the constant reminder of that covenant upon which the Father is free to bestow all active good upon me, sinner that I am. He pleads for me there. The other, my Comforter, dwells within my heart and pleads for me here. If I find myself in the "middle of a fix" he is right there with me because he is *in me*—no matter how tough the going may be. He knows the will of God and will help me find it. Between the One "up there" and the One "down here" I cannot miss the Father's way if I am sincere at all in wanting to take it. In fact, it is this triumphant assurance which breaks forth in the very next verse—though few have observed the connection—"For we *know* that to them that love God *all things* work together for good" (Rom. 8:28).

IN BIBLE READING

In the devotional study of the Bible, no less than in prayer, the Holy Spirit stands ready likewise with all needed help. I am not thinking so much now of preachers and teachers who are searching the Bible for sermons and lesson texts for their classes. It is one thing to look for sermons and quite another to nourish one's own inner life on the Word of God. But one who sits in the pew has wisely suggested that preachers and teachers would more generally feed their hungry flocks if their searching for texts and topics resolved itself more often into a quest for the satisfying of their own needs. Surely that which has not first been appropriated by the minister of the Word himself has little about it to nourish the spiritual life of those who attend his ministry.

In this discussion, however, my concern is chiefly for the many pilgrims along life's way who know that man does not live by bread alone and who hunger for God's true manna—even "the food which abideth unto eternal life" (John 6:27). No one can neglect the reading of God's Word for such a purpose without tragically falling short of his opportunities. The power inherent in the Word is released only as the Holy Spirit interprets and applies its truth to the obedient heart. The apostle Paul made this very clear in his touching farewell to his friends at Miletus. "And now," said he, "I commend you to God, and to the word of his grace, which is able to build you up, and to give you the inheritance among all them that are sanctified" (Acts 20:32). These converts newly won from their pagan ways had not yet come into their own, but Paul was confident that there was in the word of his grace a power which would not only build them up but would also make really theirs the full portion of their inheritance among all the saints.

The reading of the Bible, therefore, means very little apart from the attendant ministry of the Holy Spirit in the heart of the reader. It will remain a closed book to the man who undertakes to grasp its message by the powers of his intellect alone. Two things are necessary before the Scriptures can yield their treasures, and both of them depend absolutely upon the Spirit of God. In the first place, a man must be born of the Spirit. Without that experience he lacks the capacity for spiritual truth. He cannot even get the idea of the kingdom, as Jesus so plainly said to Nicodemus (John 3:3). "The natural man received not the things of the Spirit of God: for they are foolishness unto him: neither can he know them, because they are spiritually discerned" (1 Cor. 2:14). In the second place, a man so born must come to a point in spiritual maturity where he is thoroughly committed to the Lordship of Christ.

Disclosures in the realm of revealed truth are of such a nature that one must be guided into them. Short of a willingness to do, there can be no ability to know! The Spirit's revelation requires a willingness to follow. This attitude of will seems to be what Paul had in mind in 2 Corinthians 3:15–17. He speaks there of a veil which is taken away only when a man turns to the Lord in the once-for-allness of a true consecration.[2] It is foolishness to think that one can understand much of God's Word apart from a willingness to walk in the steps of the Guide. On the other hand, amazing indeed is the progress in a spiritual understanding of those who have said the "irrevocable yes" to Jesus. Once they were like babes needing to be fed the milk of the gospel, but after the crisis of consecration their growth to spiritual maturity is astonishingly rapid.

The experience of the Ethiopian eunuch is a case in point. As treasurer under Queen Candace he must have been a man of great ability and intelligence. There can be no question about his sincerity, for he was earnestly seeking the light. The prophecy of Isaiah from which he was reading seems to us the most easily understood of all portions of Scripture in its vivid portrayal of Christ's sufferings upon the cross. Surely under such circumstances man could come upon the truth. But when Philip asked, "Understandest thou what thou readest?" he could only reply, "How *can* I, except someone shall guide me?"

In the quest of God's truth every man needs a guide. Left to his own resources he will miss the way. In answer to

---

[2] A free translation of the passage is: "But whenever a man once really turns to the Lord, the veil is removed."

this pathetic trait of the natural mind our Lord has promised the Spirit of truth. "He shall guide you into all
truth. . . . He shall glorify me: for he shall take of mine,
and shall declare it unto you" (John 16:13–14).

Some years ago, it was my privilege in a tour of Europe,
to glimpse some of her treasures of art. There I learned
that the value of what one sees depends very largely upon
his guide. When we visited the Louvre in Paris, through
some unfortunate mistake in the arrangements, our party
had no guide. We were left utterly to our own resources.
We did the best we could, of course. We saw the "Winged
Victory," "Venus de Milo," the "Mona Lisa" and count-
less other works of art, but there was no one at hand to
refresh us with the details and the background in such a
way as to give significance to the objects which we viewed.
Many treasures we missed entirely.

In Florence a few days later, however, our experience
was quite different. There amid the priceless legacies of
the Renaissance we were blessed with the services of a good
guide. He was himself an artist, steeped in the lore of the
city. He knew the masters and the schools which followed
them. He would lead us past dozens of pictures to bring
us to the one "really good," and lingering lovingly before
it, he would revel in the message of the master and the
technique which he had perfected. The day was filled
with meaning. I learned more in art appreciation in those
two days with him than in all my life before. The guide
made the difference.

The lesson is obvious. If one is ever to appreciate the
treasures of God's Word, he must engage the services of
the Guide. Run not before him, neither lag behind. Stand
where he puts you, see what he shows you, heed what he

tells you. "He shall guide you into all the truth,"—"things which eye saw not, and ear heard not, And which entered not into the heart of man, Whatsoever things God prepared for them that love him . . . unto us God revealed them through the Spirit" (1 Cor. 2:9–10).

Dr. A. T. Robertson was one of the greatest teachers I ever had. His monumental *Grammar of the Greek New Testament,* a book of more than fourteen hundred pages, marked an epoch in New Testament scholarship and has become a standard in its field. It was my privilege to study this book under him. No one was better qualified to teach it than he, the man who wrote it. I have often thought how this exactly duplicates our position with reference to the greatest Book of all. It is our privilege to study the Bible under the personal tutelage and in the intimate fellowship of the One who wrote it.

It is only natural that we feel ourselves at a loss when we compare our lot with that of the disciples of old who kept company with Jesus. How we envy them the privilege which was theirs! They could hear him teach and watch as he performed his wonders. Best of all, they could turn to him with their perplexities and questions. But there is a subtle temptation in this frame of mind. Almost unaware we excuse ourselves for our ignorance of things spiritual. We ignore him who has come to teach us all things (John 14:26), and we disbelieve the plain word of Jesus who said, "It is *expedient for you* that I go away: for if I go not away, the Comforter will not come unto you; but if I depart, I will send him unto you" (John 16:7).

Instead of being at a disadvantage in comparison with the disciples who followed Jesus when he was here upon earth, quite the contrary is the case. We are just as free to go to the Holy Spirit with our perplexities as ever they were to go to him. And the answers are just as sure to be forthcoming. Indeed, as we witness the mighty miracles of Jesus, we have this distinct advantage. The Holy Spirit gives us the point of view and the interpretation which most of the onlookers in that day missed entirely. We must remember that he was not only an eyewitness of all that took place, but also the very agent by whose power these things happened. If we but let him, he will help us to reconstruct the scene so as to receive its richest values. Such is the charm and challenge of reading the Scriptures with an awareness of his presence who recorded them for our admonition unto whom the end of the ages are come!

The ministry of the Holy Spirit in relation to the believer and the Word of God may be summed up in three words: illumination, application, and appropriation. He supplies illumination by revealing its meaning to us. He makes application by convicting us of our condition in the light of its truth. He inspires appropriation by quickening its promises to challenge our faith. He did this for Jesus in his temptation (Matt. 4:4), and he will do it for us. This is the Word men live by—not the Word written and recorded long ago, but the Word which under the Spirit's quickening *"proceedeth* [note the tense] out of the mouth of God."

In order to encourage a deeper and stronger devotional life, a great denomination publishes a magazine of daily devotional helps called *Open Windows.* The title is a happy one. It reminds the reader of Daniel, one of God's most beloved and useful servants whose open window was the secret of his marvelous life. His long ministry, his courage and devotion, his insight into hidden meanings, and his profound understanding of God's purposes as they were to unfold through successive ages—all stem from the fact that even under threat of death he opened his window toward Jerusalem and prayed. We may well follow his example. Our devotional life will take on new strength and meaning when we open the windows of the soul toward the new Jerusalem and let the quickening breath of God's Holy Spirit fan the fires that slumber on the altar within into a brightly burning flame.

IV

His Ministry of Comfort

Of all the names and titles by which the third person of the Trinity is known, none carries more precious insight into his nature and his work, and none commends him more warmly to us than that given to him by the Lord Jesus—the Comforter. One might almost say that "Holy Spirit" tells us *what* he is while "Comforter" tells us *who* he is. If this distinction holds true, it seems almost a pity that we use the terms Holy Spirit or Holy Ghost all but exclusively in our references to him. After all, one does not warm up readily to a spirit, let alone a ghost! We are more like "Hambone" than we care to admit. He said, "Maybe there haint no ghosts but ma' laigs don't 'low me to take no chances!" But this difficulty vanishes when we think of the Comforter. There is something warm and real and personal about that name which brings him near to us in an intimate and tender way.

In that darkest of all nights when Jesus was about to be

taken from them, the disciples must have welcomed the promise, "I will pray the Father, and he shall give you another Comforter. . . . I will not leave you desolate [orphans]" (John 14:16, 18). We cling to that promise now in a world where the waves of sin and sorrow, death and destruction would still overwhelm us.

> O spread the tidings 'round, wherever man is found,
> Wherever human hearts and human woes abound;
>
> . . . .
> The Comforter has come!
>
> F. BOTTOME

The meaning of this word "Comforter" is so rich that we must give it special attention. The variety of ways in which the term and its cognates are translated in the New Testament bears eloquent testimony to its rich content. In 1 John 2:1, it is translated "Advocate"—"And if any man sin, we have an *Advocate* with the Father, Jesus Christ the righteous." Anyone familiar with legal proceedings will appreciate the force of this figure. While the Son is now at the Father's right hand pleading our case, the Spirit is here, in the midst of our troubled circumstances, speaking a word of cheer and interceding likewise for us, defending us at the bar of our own conscience from the accusations of Satan.

Many times, as in Hebrews 10:25, the verb built upon this same stem is translated "exhort"; *"Exhorting* one another."* The obvious meaning here is one of encouragement. The actual word "encourage" is not used in our English New Testament, but the idea is there many times over. In Acts 4:36 the kindly Barnabas had become so imbued with the Holy Spirit that he was affectionately dubbed "Son of consolation" (encouragement). How well he lived up to this nickname may be seen in the way he championed Saul, the newly converted Pharisee, and John Mark, the young man who had once turned back from the open door of opportunity. Thus, when failures arise out of the past to threaten our own self-confidence and that of others in us, the Comforter comes to our rescue with words of encouragement.

The new Revised Standard Version of the New Testament uses "Counselor" by way of translation. That is good as far as it goes, but it is not warm enough, not flexible enough to do justice to the idea which our Lord must have had in mind. But though Counselor, Paraclete, Helper, Encourager, Friend-near-at-hand would all do well as translations of the Greek term, I still prefer the choice made by the editors of the King James and the American Revised versions. We cannot do better than "Comforter." That is the idea in 2 Corinthians 1:3–8 where the word occurs nine times. Primarily it is God's comfort and encouragement that the Spirit applies to his children in the hour of their distress.

Since translations are so varied, we shall do well to look at the word itself. *Paraclātos*, the Greek word which is transliterated *Paraclete* and translated Comforter, is a compound of the preposition *para* which means "along by," and a verbal substantive from *kaleo* which means to "call." The idea is the help of "someone calling (or called) alongside" in time of need. The picture in this wonderful word was dramatized for me by an incident that happened some years ago within my own family circle.

There had been a football game between the midget teams of rival high schools. My youngest son, Jack, was one of the players, and another son, David, was an ardent supporter of the home team. Due to an out-of-town engagement I had to miss this classic battle of the midgets. In telling me about it, a friend of mine described a play in which Jack ran almost the length of the field for a touchdown. "The interesting thing about it," he said, "was to see the way David was pulling for him. As Jack made the run, David also ran alongside the boundary, actually beating him to the goal line, cheering and shouting encouragement." As the friend laughingly described the scene to me, God seemed to say, "There you have it. That's the perfect picture in the word Paraclete. Thus do I in the person of the Comforter give every encouragement and assistance while you run the race set before you."

Such an idea, though much more complete and wonderful, must have been in the mind of Jesus when he chose this name for the Holy Spirit. Then, as now, he was tremendously concerned with the "morale" of his disciples. Many times while with them he had encouraged them to be of good cheer. Now he was to be taken from them. Their way would be dark and difficult. Discouragement with its gloom would settle upon them. His answer was the Paraclete. "I will not leave you comfortless". . ."I will pray the Father, and he shall give you another Comforter" (John 14:18, 16). The difference then and now between dejected, downcast, discouraged disciples and cheerful, courageous, radiant followers of Jesus is a difference measured in terms of response to the Holy Spirit's ministry of comfort.

We shall now see how beautifully the Spirit lives up to this title through his dealings with God's children in their many trials and tribulations.

THE ASSURANCE OF SONSHIP

One outstanding contribution the Spirit of God makes is to assure us of our sonship. On the wings of assurance he bears us up to a position of dignity and to a frame of mind which befits the child of God. "The Spirit himself beareth witness with our spirit, that we are children of God: and if children, then heirs; heirs of God, and joint-heirs with Christ; if so be that we suffer with him, that we may be also glorified with him" (Rom. 8:16–17).

Right here I would sound a preliminary caution. In our eagerness for the assurance of sonship we are in danger of reading this passage carelessly. There are many who take it to read: "The Spirit himself beareth witness *to* our spirit." But such is not the case. He bears witness *with* our spirit that we are the children of God. There is a vast difference. Our spirits must make the assertion of sonship which strikes the responsive chord with God, who follows with his affirmation.

Bearing witness with us, he says the "Amen." I make this point because the quest for comfort can be a tremendously selfish thing. Usually it is. When sorrow first comes, quite naturally we give way to our emotions. We lie prostrate, completely overwhelmed by our grief. Friends come to our aid with that sweet balm of Gilead which we call sympathy. They pour forth their compassion; we become the center of concern. Almost before we know it we accept our position in the center of the picture as right and normal. The sorrow still is great, but there are compensations. Everything turns around us—*our* affliction and *our* grief, *our* desires and *our* comforts! We like the attention; it's the thing we have been missing for some time. Or, lacking

he sympathy from others, we try to make up for it by pity-
ng ourselves. Such self-centeredness, of course, cannot but
grieve God and become the occasion of our further undoing.

I do not know how far my observation may be sustained
by others more competent in this field of ministry, but I
have often felt that much of the sympathy we give is misguided. Too often it is soft and sentimental, lacking in
discernment. Instead of gently leading the sufferer to rely
on God and to draw upon the inner resources of his grace,
this perverted sympathy tends to increase his dependence
upon ourselves (thus incidentally and quite significantly
magnifying our own importance) or upon other "props"
equally harmful both to body and mind.

Remember that God's great purpose in affliction is to
effect a maturity like that shown by Paul who said, "I have
learned in whatsoever state I am, therein to be content
[self-sufficient]" (Phil. 4:11). God would wean us from
dependence upon our surroundings and human associates
to the independence of being utterly dependent upon him.
In the darkest hour, when circumstances render the Christian powerless to act, he can at least *affirm his sonship*.
Out of the gloom will come, unmistakably, the voice of the
Spirit confirming that claim and encouraging him to appropriate with a free hand the wealth that such a heritage
means.

But, getting back to the main theme in Romans 8:16–
7, all of us need the encouragement that comes from this
blessed assurance of sonship. I suppose it is true that much
of our trouble is derived from an exaggerated idea of our
own importance. But I am certain that much of it also
comes from a haunting sense of inferiority. Our boastful-

ness and daring insolence is often but a screen to hide from ourselves, and we hope from others, our own feeling of shameful inadequacy. The success others seem to have achieved contributes to our sense of frustration. We are getting nowhere at all in life's mad race. We have been pushed about with such high-minded contempt that we feel ourselves unappreciated "nobodies"—miserable victims in the fell clutch of circumstance. Life's cup has been made bitter by the dregs of our own failure.

Herein lies the secret of discouragement, and to it God has a sure answer. He wants you to know that in spite of your failure, regardless of the way your circumstances may be interpreted against you, you *are* somebody—you are *his child.* This is the comfort that the Holy Spirit brings. Sustained by such assurance you may lift up your head and bear your sorrow with the quiet dignity that bespeaks victory within. God is your Father, and with Jesus Christ his Son who has suffered, too, you are the triumphant heir of all things.

This assurance is one of the sweetest consolations in life. I have known it on the human level both as son and father. There is something in it satisfying beyond words. Tears streaming through the dirt on his chubby cheeks, a small boy comes running to his father, crying for the comfort he is certain to receive. How will the father respond? He will gather him into his strong arms and brushing away the tears will say, "There, there now, everything's all right, son. You're daddy's little man; that's what you are, you're daddy's fine boy. Don't cry any more."

We do not analyze such experiences, though all of us have had them. But stopping now to look back upon them in the light of this passage, do you not see in the running of the child to his father a claim to sonship? Do you not also see in the response of the father an affirmation of that claim? He acknowledges a relationship for which he alone stands responsible, which also is the guarantee of all the assistance that is within his power to give. Thus our Father in heaven speaks to us when, hurt by the hard things of life, we turn to him. In his witness with our spirit that we are the children of God, the Holy Spirit lifts us by divine logic out of our sense of inferiority into the dignity of one who gladly suffers with his fellow-Heir in order likewise to be glorified with him.

> A tent or a cottage, why should I care?
> They're building a palace for me over there;
> Tho' exiled from home, yet still I may sing:
> All glory to God, I'm a child of the King.
>   HATTIE E. BUELL

The next time you are discouraged try singing the words of this hymn. As you do you will find the Spirit accompanies your affirmation of faith with the music of heaven.

THE MEANING OF AFFLICTION

On the night before his crucifixion, in our Lord's conversation with his disciples where so much is said about the "other Comforter," he explains: "I have yet many things to say unto you, but ye cannot bear them now. Howbeit when he, the Spirit of truth, is come, he shall guide you into all truth" (John 16:12–13). At that time the vast wealth of God's gospel of love was yet to be revealed. The substance of it was given later through the apostles in the New Testament as we have it today. But the application of that individual love was then and is now something the Holy Spirit must work out with every believer.

Only thus is it possible for each to receive his portion in due season (Luke 12:42).

The necessity for this individual approach is especially true in the case of suffering. This problem is so great that only the Spirit of God is capable of interpreting it. Those who run in before him and undertake to give their own explanation will earn from the sufferer the just rebuke of Job: "I have heard many such things: miserable comforters are ye all" (Job 16:2). In my experience as pastor I have found no master key to the problem of suffering except that which the sovereign Spirit carries in his hand. I know this:

> Blind unbelief is sure to err
> And scan His work in vain.
> *God is his own interpreter*
> *And He will make it plain.*
>   WILLIAM COWPER

Almost the first and always the inevitable cry wrung from the heart of any sufferer is the word, *"Why?"* It is one of the most maddening questions in human experience. Even Jesus cried in agony from the cross, "My God, my God, *why!*" Men not only suffer from a sense of inferiority and inadequacy, but also from frustration, from the uselessness and the apparent meaninglessness of their distress. Counting the cost, they look for the gain. They weigh their effort and toil over against the failures and blasted hopes and strike no balance. Things do not add up. There is neither rhyme nor reason. They are mocked by that most paralyzing of all questions, "What's the use?" It is the sense of futility that makes many a situation unbearable.

Just at this point the Holy Spirit proves himself a Comforter by the meaning he assigns to all the experiences of life, especially our afflictions. He is God's great Interpreter. The reader of Bunyan's immortal allegory, *The Pilgrim's Progress,* will recall how Christian in his journey from the City of Destruction to the Celestial City came to the House of the Interpreter. The rooms of that house were filled with strange sights which at once baffled and intrigued the visitor. In each instance the Interpreter explained the meaning to the mystified pilgrim, drawing lessons from the experience which stood him in good stead throughout the remainder of his journey. God goes Bunyan one better. His Interpreter does not dwell in a house beside the way. There is, therefore, no need for the pilgrim to take grateful leave of him in order to continue his journey toward the Celestial City. God's Interpreter goes with him, walking at his side, unfolding the highest meaning in each mystifying experience until he comes to the end of the way.

We need to recognize that life is made up of situations, one after another—some "good," some "bad." We are no sooner out of one set of circumstances than we are into another. We need to recognize also that these situations are capable of an endless variety of constructions. We need to recognize, further, that the level of our living will be determined by the construction that we adopt. This matter of interpretation, therefore, is of utmost importance. Like the physician, if we fail in our diagnosis of a case, we will inevitably come up with the wrong treatment.

In the main there are three levels of interpretation from which we may choose. The first is the devil's base and malicious slander. In his effort to make us renounce our faith, he construes everything in such a way as to put God in the worst possible light. The second level is the counsel of well-meaning but short-sighted friends. Because most of them are blind to spiritual values, their theories and explanations are often of more use to the Slanderer than they are to God. The third and highest possible level is the meaning the Holy Spirit gives to a situation through the grace of God in Christ Jesus. This is revealed to the eye of faith alone.

Included in his counsel are the things which for sheer goodness lie beyond the fondest reach of human imagination. But unto us God reveals them through the Spirit, and happy is he who hath ears to hear and heart to heed the higher testimony of this Friend and Counselor. For him life opens up with new and blessed meaning.

The path that Jesus walked was on this highest level. It is interesting to study the constructions which he gave to life's encounters. As an example, consider his reaction to the news of Lazarus' illness. "The sisters therefore sent unto him saying, Lord, behold, he whom thou lovest is sick" (John 11:3). Immediately the Spirit gave him to know what the Father's intention was in it. "This sickness," he said, "is not unto death, but for the glory of God, that the Son of God may be glorified thereby" (John 11:4). Having taken this position through this declaration of faith, he stood by it to find a glorious vindication in the results which followed. The highest possible meaning that could be brought out of Lazarus' sickness and death and out of all the suspense, the misunderstanding and heartache of his sisters was to be found in the interpretation which Jesus gave it. The path which he trod is the one we are to follow.

Our problem is simplified once we find God's meaning.
Faith rests in the quiet confidence that God's purposes are
worth all they cost. "The Son can do nothing of himself,
but . . . the Father loveth the Son, *and showeth him all
things*" (John 5:19-20). And the Father's way of revealing
"all things" to us is through the ministry of the Holy Spirit,
our great interpreter.

Two women, patients in a hospital ward, were overheard
discussing their respective physicians. "I like my doctor
just fine," one said to the other. "He takes the time to
explain what is going on and what he is trying to do. That
makes the pain easier to bear." Then after a slight pause
the sufferer continued, "I can stand anything if I know it's
helping me to get well." The Holy Spirit is like that
physician. If we listen to him, he will explain, if not all,
at least enough of the treatment to help us bear the pain in
the full assurance that God knows what he is about.

The Word of God is replete with interpretations which
the Holy Spirit gives to our trials. Only he can answer the
searching heart and match the need with the particular
Word that cleanses and heals. Sometimes he may whisper,
"It is for chastening that ye endure; God dealeth with you
as with sons" (Heb. 12:7). Then you will know that your
affliction, so far from meaning that God has cast you off
and forgotten you, is an evidence of your sonship and of a
Father's loving care. In this process of bringing many sons
to glory even the Author of salvation did not escape. He
was made perfect through suffering (Heb. 2:10). Would it
not, then, be strange indeed if you were to escape entirely?

> When through fiery trials thy pathway shall lie,
> My grace, all sufficient, shall be thy supply;

The flame shall not hurt thee;—I only design
Thy dross to consume, and thy gold to refine.

GEORGE KEITH

At other times his interpretation of trouble may not b
so plain. If after carefully searching your heart in the ligh
of the Word, you still can find no occasion within yoursel
for the affliction, then the Great Interpreter may want yo
to look out upon God's larger purpose. He may point yo
to a man like Job, whose uprightness of character mad
him a target for the enemy's cruelest attack. A necessar
part of Job's magnificent victory was the fact that he coul
not see all that was going on. He could only trust. Eve
though the Spirit cannot for the moment show you th
whole sweep of God's design, he assures you that Go
knows, God cares, God loves, and God overrules. Whe
this is the case, all must be well. A wise and loving purpos
lies behind all the suffering God permits. The Spirit point
us to his own interpretation and gives us both the faith t
take it and the courage to follow it on out to the end
Vindication will come, even though we must abide ou
time.

> Not till each loom is silent
>   And the shuttles cease to fly,
> Will God reveal the pattern
>   And explain the reason why
>
> The dark threads were as needful
>   In the Weaver's skilful hand
> As the threads of gold and silver
>   For the pattern which He planned.

AUTHOR UNKNOWN

THE AWARENESS OF A PRESENCE

But the greatest comfort of all is found in the awareness of God's presence. "I will not leave you desolate, I come unto you" (John 14:18). "Lo, I am with you always, even unto the end of the world" (Matt. 28:20). Here is God's supreme answer to the trials and tribulations of this life. He cannot remove them and at the same time accomplish his purposes of grace. But he can and he does share them. He enters into them with us, and that is far better than removing them. In the experience of the believer, it is profoundly true:

> I would rather walk in the dark with God
>   than go alone in the light;
> I would rather walk with Him by faith than
>   walk alone by sight.
>   MARY GARDINER BRAINARD

This sharing with us in life's joys and sorrows is the climax of God's benediction. "The grace of the Lord Jesus Christ, and the love of God, and the communion [fellowship] of the Holy Spirit be with you all" (2 Cor. 13:14). The Holy Spirit is here, in our midst, in the very thick of our trials. He has cast his lot with us and stands ready to abide by the position he has taken. Wherever we are, he is, for he has made of our bodies his temple (1 Cor. 6:19). Not just the strong bodies, mind you, but our sick bodies also—with all their aches and pains!

Herein lies the remedy to one of the greatest causes of human grief—that sense of aloneness which so often becomes all but insufferable. It is the tendency both of sin and sickness to isolate. Sin reverses the telescope and putting the larger end to the eye makes God appear a long

way off. And though we are not dealing primarily here
with sin, or the suffering necessarily traceable to sin, the
hangover of our former heritage as sinners is a real factor
which we must face. It is natural, therefore, for us to feel
that God has forsaken us when trouble comes. Affliction
sets us apart from others. It detains us from our accustomed
round. It lays us on the shelf of inactivity. The busy world
goes on without us and we are left alone—forgotten, it
would seem, by God and man, a burden to ourselves and
others.

This is not an imagined line of reasoning. It is the actual
path by which physical distress becomes mental, adding its
tortures to those of a sick body and multiplying them a
thousand times over. It is the subtle insinuation of Satan.
"No sorrow is like your sorrow," he says. "No one understands or cares. What's the use! Renounce God and die."
And even though one may refuse to believe him, the
torment of his insinuation lingers.

Let me repeat, the comfort God gives to those who suffer
from this sense of aloneness is that of his own presence
and the one who makes us aware of that presence is the
Holy Spirit. God's children triumph over adversity and
confound their adversaries through the awareness that he
is near. When he becomes manifest, the victory is won.
"Lo," said king Nebuchadnezzar, "I see four men loose,
walking in the midst of the fire, and they have no hurt,
and the aspect of the fourth is like a son of the gods" (Dan.
3:25). As in the days of the three Hebrew children, so now
it is God's glory to enter into such an experience with us.
His presence makes all the difference.

You recall how the fearful disciples once earned a rebuke
from the Master when their ship was threatened by a rag-

ing sea. In stark terror they woke him from his sleep with the reproach, "Carest thou not that we perish?" (Mark 4:38). Looking back upon it we argue however rough the elements were, there was, in fact, nothing for them to fear so long as their Master was with them in the boat.

> Whether the wrath of the storm-tossed sea,
> Or demons, or men, or whatever it be,
> No water can swallow the ship where lies
> The Master of ocean and earth and skies.
>
> MARY A. BAKER

It is easy for us to see where their faith failed, but it is difficult to apply the lesson in our own case when storms break upon us. The Holy Spirit is in the same boat with us. He is with us even more intimately than Jesus was with them, for he actually dwells in us. Why be alarmed and encourage our fears by looking at the rough elements when we can look on the tranquil face of the Master who so graciously rides the storm with us?

The sense of God's presence will bring rest to troubled hearts and relaxation to nerves drawn tense by anxiety. When the burden of care was proving too much even for a rugged man like Moses, God gave him a promise, "My presence shall go with thee, and I will give thee rest" (Ex. 33:14). There between himself and Moses God revealed a principle which works wherever there is love for and confidence in another.

Many years ago a flaxen-haired little girl of two lay sleeping in the crib by her mother's bed. Her preacher-father had moved to a new field and she was in strange surroundings. For some reason she awoke in the night and her big blue eyes tried in vain to pierce the darkness and find comfort in something familiar. Finally a small hand reached out between the bars of her little crib to rest gently upon her mother. And then a childish voice broke the stillness of the night: "Mamma, are that you?" "Yes, my child," replied the mother, instantly awake. Then, "Mamma, are this me," "Yes, my precious, that is you," replied the mother. Then silence as the little one finding rest in the presence of one whom she loved and trusted fell soundly asleep. In the same way the Holy Spirit brings rest to God's weary child by making him aware of the presence of One whom he loves and trusts.

Let me close this chapter about the Holy Spirit and his ministry of comfort with a personal testimony. There is nothing like trouble to reveal the worth of our friends. They are summoned by our need and tried by our adversity. In the time of tragedy or bereavement they flock to us. We are surprised by their number and humbled by their kindness. Their presence is a testimony to God's comforting Spirit reaching out through them to us. There is compensation in the experience that draws them to us. We are enriched by their fellowship. It is that way with God and it is worth all that trouble may cost us to get to know him better.

The first time that death invaded our family circle was when one of my brothers was taken. But he died in faraway China, and I was here in the States. I did not know of the illness which took him until three weeks after his burial. I wept at the news of his going, but my heart was not crushed. It was quite different when Mother went. I was at her bedside. No loss had overtaken me like this. Because of my great love for her I had expected to be prostrated with grief when the end came. But such was not the case. In her going I came to know the Comforter as I had never known him before. It was all very quiet and inexpressibly sweet. To my grateful surprise I felt myself borne along through all the trying adjustments and the final triumphant farewell at the graveside. And the thing that impressed me most about that comfort was its *within-ness*. In the person of his great Spirit, God was tenderly bearing me up, interpreting my sorrow in terms of Christ's resurrection victory and making mine the quiet joy of his own wondrous presence. And this also I know, in all essential elements my experience differs in no way from that of multiplied thousands whose serenity in time of stress and sorrow bears eloquent testimony that *the Comforter has come.*

V

The Supply of the Spirit

The great majority of Christ's followers today know the importance of service and have sensed something of the joys that may be found in it. Christians readily agree that serving is their one great business as it was their Lord's, who came "not to be ministered unto, but to minister" (Matt. 20:28). They are busy enough. Indeed, there is ceaseless, almost feverish activity of an undoubtedly well-meaning nature. A study of the announcements in almost any church bulletin reveals many such "activities"—multiplied almost to the breaking point of those who seriously take part in them. The urge to serve is seen in civic clubs and social organizations as well as in the church. But to the thoughtful observer something is wrong. "Where does it get us?" he asks, and, more thoughtfully yet, "Where does it get others?"

The painful answer is that so much of what we call "service" proves ineffectual. The tree is full of leaves, but little fruit abides. Unhappily, a great portion of our activity falls under the classification of "dead works." The truth is that the vitalizing touch of the Holy Spirit is missing from our busy life. In the realm of service he is our supreme helper, and our ministry as well as our devotional life must be energized by him.

A word picture in Philippians 1:19 illustrates this aspect of the Holy Spirit's ministry. As he writes, the apostle Paul is in prison at Rome awaiting trial. He is uncertain what the outcome may be but finds occasion to rejoice in the fact that all that has happened to him thus far has turned out to the progress of the gospel. He is sure that the whole experience will, as he puts it, "turn out to my salvation, through your supplication and the *supply of the Spirit* of Jesus Christ."

The idea in the Greek word *epichoragia*, translated "supply," throws a wealth of light on the way the Holy Spirit helps us in a life of service. Our English word "chorus" is derived from it. The history of the word extends all the way back to the drama in the days of ancient Greece. The chorus was the cast of players who put on the performance. Because this form of entertainment was expensive, usually some public-spirited citizen of means would bear the cost, supplying the varied needs of the cast so that the play could be presented without admission charge. It was the supply of this generous patron of the arts that made the performance possible. His wealth stood back of the undertaking. In the course of time the word came to mean "supply."

When one thinks of a performance like that put on by a huge circus, he instantly becomes aware of the varied and great demands created by the needs of such a troupe. Somewhere behind this "greatest show on earth" the matter of supply must be carefully worked out: in degree as the show is large, and in kind as the show is varied. Wherever the circus goes, and under whatever conditions it performs, the matter of supply is indispensable. The same thing is obvious in the strategy of war. Who can project a mighty task force converging upon an enemy stronghold without first solving the problems of supply? No general will adopt tactics which put his troops beyond the effective supply of their needs.

The history of this word affords us a wonderful insight into the operation of the Spirit of Jesus Christ. Wherever we are called to serve, under any and all conditions, God guarantees the adequate supply of our every need through the One who dwells within us. That is the wealth of meaning with which this figure is fraught.

But before we leave this passage in Philippians, observe that Paul says, "through your supplication *and* the supply of the Spirit of Jesus Christ." In most cases the Holy Spirit does not supply our needs independently of others. As we saw in a previous chapter, it is his comfort—not less but more—when it comes to us through others of God's children in whom he dwells and through whom he works. Sometimes his "supplies" of grace are imparted to us with a directness which seems almost to preclude human channels and agencies. At other times he shares the joy and the glory of his ministry with others by operating through them. It was the Spirit of God who first laid the burden of prayer for Paul upon the hearts of the Philippians, and his "salvation" from the trying ordeal of imprisonment was all the more wonderful on this account. We need a deeper appreciation of what God is doing through others in whom he works his good pleasure. Members of the body of Christ have this happy relationship to one another. In another passage (Eph. 4:16) Paul speaks of "that which every joint supplieth." The word is the same. It is all the supply of the Spirit.

The Holy Spirit will supply God's child with everything that is needed to make his service to the Lord Jesus complete and acceptable. That is a bold statement to make, but it needs no qualification. He is himself the full and sufficient equipment for service. If such is his sovereign pleasure, he will supply the physical needs of God's servants independently of means known to man. This is what he did for an army of more than two million souls who wandered forty years in a "waste and howling wilderness." The name of their food was manna—"what is it?" (Ex. 16:15). So far as the wisdom of man is concerned that question has never been answered from that day to this. Their drink, too, was from a spiritual source, from a "spiritual rock that followed them" (1 Cor. 10:4). Elijah partook of a meal which, so far as we know, was not prepared by human hands and went in the strength of it forty days and forty nights (1 Kings 19:6, 8). Philip, worn from a long journey southward to find the Ethiopian eunuch, and traveling yet further with him as he rode in his chariot, was supplied return transportation by the Spirit alone who delivered him in a rapture of bliss at Azotus (Acts 8:40).

I labor this point because we are naturally slow to grasp the truth that reality lies in the spiritual realm, not the physical. But surely, if we believe in the fact of creation we must believe that this material world about us had its origin in the invisible realm of the spirit. It is foolish, then, for us to limit the resources of the Spirit to things we can see and sense. He who is the source of our supply is both Creator and Sustainer of our world.

But the problem of effective service is not primarily one of material equipment. It goes far deeper than that. Conditions on the outside are usually the least of our worries. Something needs to happen on the inside that will transform our ministry from one of dead works to one of fruit that abides. That something is accomplished only by the life-giving Spirit of God. Let us examine how he works within to vitalize the service we seek to impart. From this approach 2 Timothy 1:7 becomes most illuminating. "For God gave us not a spirit of fearfulness; but of power and love and discipline." If we spell the word "spirit" with a capital "S" and use "sober-mindedness" as an alternate translation for "discipline," we shall see how the Holy Spirit supplies to effective service the three essentials: motive, wisdom, and power.

THE MOTIVE

Motive means everything with God who declares himself quick to discern the thoughts and intents of the heart (Heb. 4:12). It means everything with others, also, who have an uncanny way of seeing what lies back of all that we do and say. Furthermore, in the matter of motive it is far easier for us to deceive ourselves than others. That is why the help of the Holy Spirit at this point is so necessary. He gets back to the mainspring of effort and supplies the proper motivation.

Love is, of course, the motive that prompts all effectual service. It is the one thing necessary, giving value to all else. "If I speak with the tongues of men and of angels, but have not love, I am become sounding brass, or clanging cymbal. And if I have the gift of prophecy, and know all mysteries and all knowledge; and if I have all faith, so as to remove mountains, but have not love, I am nothing. And if I bestow all my goods to feed the poor, and if I give my body to be burned, but have not love, it profiteth me nothing" (1 Cor. 13:1–3). Here the apostle lists the most precious gifts that adorn a Christian ministry and declares them all without consequence apart from love. We are slow to realize how much of what we do or say is charged off by the world around us as "sounding brass and clanging cymbal"—a loveless gesture which mocks rather than meets the needs of hungry hearts.

Our great programs of service are weak in their motivation. We do not love. We act from impure motives. The fear of man, the desire for approbation (especially in our own set), a false standard of success, the pressure of circumstances—all cripple the effectiveness of our deeds by striking at that which prompts them. Our hearts are cramped and straightened by our own prejudices and self-interests. Our efforts are often doomed to failure from the very start. Of course, we have love of a sort. But it is love that centers about self. We love those who love us, but that is all. Little that we do is marked with joyous abandon, the spontaneity of pure love. We do not have motivation strong enough or worthy enough to prompt a life of noble service. Sin has perverted our love-life by making self the center and not Christ.

No one knows our destitution in this respect better than God, and the way that he has met our needs through the indwelling Spirit is marvelous beyond words. The simple and glorious truth is that when God came into our hearts to live, he brought with him his love as well. How could it be otherwise if God is love? John speaks of "the love which God hath in us" (1 John 4:16). The love which he has in us is the same as that which he has for us.

The difference between his love and ours is manifest in two respects. His is the kind that loves first. "We love, because he *first* loved us" (1 John 4:19). Turn now to Romans 5:6, 8, 10 and underscore the phrases, "yet weak . . . yet sinners . . . enemies." Unlovely as we were, Christ died for us. There was nothing about us to provoke his love. It was entirely free and spontaneous, and when it finds an outlet through us, it will be the same sort. We, too, will love those who are in themselves unlovely. The second mark of that love is its willingness to go the full length of devotion. Jesus, having loved his own, loved them unto the uttermost (John 13:1, margin). The love of God stops short of no sacrifice. It bears the print of the nails. Such is the love that the Holy Spirit would weave into our daily experience to become the motive of Christian service.

The fifth verse in the same chapter of Romans explains how the Spirit makes God's wonderful love effective in us. "The love of God hath been shed abroad [literally poured out] in our hearts through the Holy Spirit which was given unto us." Love is not a thing that we can coerce or induce by self-effort. Much as we deplore our lack of it, we cannot generate it in our own strength. But we can open our hearts to become the channels through which God's love, bubbling up from within, will overflow to bless the world. And that is the meaning of the word "poured out." All we need to do is to recognize the inadequacy of our own love and to draw upon God's. The Holy Spirit himself is our never-failing source of supply.

A generation ago Paul's figure of a spring of water was

perhaps more readily appreciated than now. Wells were more important to people then than they seem today. It very often happened that a good well of water became of no use because sediment and debris had filled in above the water level. The well had to be cleaned out so that the water could run again, clear and fresh and sweet. That is what is needed in many a Christian life. God's children must follow the example of Isaac, who cleaned out the wells that his father Abraham had dug. When this is done, the waters of God's great love will come bubbling up from within to enrich our lives and ministry and overflow to others.

Some years ago there was such a well-cleaning in my own life. I had been with a little group of fellow pastors in a retreat for two or three days. We prayed some and talked much about the things of God. In our midst and taking the lead in the discussion was a man of a wonderfully rich love-life. In the freeness and the greatness of the love which he manifested I became convicted of my own hardness of heart and cramped compassions.

As our time together drew to its close and we were about to have a final prayer I interrupted the proceedings and made a statement regarding the things that troubled me. I said that so far as I knew there was no particular issue in my life with which God had a controversy but that there was a lot of tightness and hypocrisy within, and coldness towards God and others which indicated a lack of love. I stated that then and there I was laying down anything that might hinder me from entering into the best Jesus had for me. It was not a scheduled utterance, and I was rather surprised and embarrassed that I had spoken out in that fashion, and so, I believe, were the others, who hardly knew what to reply. That closed the incident—I thought. But it was a well-cleaning with far more joyous results than I could have anticipated.

After returning home that same afternoon, I was walking down the street—busy with matters of daily living, purely routine. I was not aware of any conscious, Godward effort or act of appropriation, but, to borrow John Wesley's famous phrase, I found my heart "strangely warmed" and myself all but overwhelmed with the consciousness that God loved me. Suddenly I realized that he loved me with a *perfect* love, and with *all* that he was. I knew that it was a perfect love for had I been left out of that love, it would have been, by just so much as I am, less than perfect! It was a veritable baptism of love. I seemed lifted up by it and swept along as in the great gulf stream of God's affection. Never before had there been such an awareness that God loved me, even *me!* And as that awareness dawned upon me there came with it the assurance that nothing else mattered. If God loved me like that, what else *could* matter! But this love did not stop with me. It was overflowing to others. I loved everybody. As I met people on the street my heart went out to them and I could scarcely restrain the impulse to put my arms about them and tell them I loved them, and far better than that, that God loved them in the same way he loved me, and that in the light of that glorious fact nothing else could matter.

The glow of this experience lingered for some days. The people in prayer meeting that night could tell a difference, though there was no demonstration. There was a liberty and a sweetness about our fellowship, the memory of which has continued like a benediction. In my preaching the following Sunday there was an abandon and freedom I had not known before. With the passing days the thrill wore off and my emotions subsided. I was not aware then, nor am I now, of any sin or disobedience that caused it to be so. It was not a shock to find that the remainder of my pilgrimage could not all be upon the mountaintop.

But although the ecstacy subsided, the lessons from this experience have not left me. At least I have glimpsed my surroundings through love-lit eyes, and things are different. I know that every contact can be made glorious and fruitful through love. God's love can find expression through the tone of one's voice, through the glance of the eye, through smile or gesture, to melt the heart and draw men to himself. I have known that God can and will love men through me. I have known that love is something not to be pretended, that in seasons of barrenness all that is needed is to clean out the well and let the love of God through his indwelling Presence come bubbling up with life and salvation in its blessed overflow. It is his love that never fails, and it is this compelling, winning love that the Holy Spirit stands ready to shed abroad in our hearts as the mainspring in a life of service.

THE WISDOM

But love is not enough. It may be and often is misguided. However sincere a man's motives may be, there are times when the big question is not *why* but *how*. Time and time again the servant of God will feel his need of wisdom. Solomon felt it and voiced a prayer which God from his very nature can never refuse: "Give me now *wisdom* and knowledge" (2 Chron. 1:10). If we take seriously the work God has given us to do, we shall soon recognize how inadequate is our own store of knowledge.

Circumstances will teach us if we do not have humility enough to know it from the start. How short-sighted and foolish we are! The mistakes that grow out of our folly are tragic indeed. In spite of the fact that God has said, "Lean not unto thine own understanding" (Prov. 3:5, KJV), we have run ahead of him. Because we rely on previous experience and human judgment instead of upon him we are covered in the shame of our own confusion and failure. But God waits in patience until we are ready to let him direct. His Spirit will supply wisdom for the task.

We have already had occasion to refer to the Holy Spirit's work as guide and interpreter. It is refreshing to think as we face a difficult task that he stands ready *to show us how.* The book of Acts is replete with instances of the Spirit's power to direct. In fact, the Christian enterprise was all new to the apostles. The Saviour's directions had been of a general nature. He had outlined their work as witnessing—to begin in Jerusalem and to extend through Judea and Samaria to the uttermost parts of the earth. But the specific steps of their procedure were left for the Holy Spirit to reveal as the occasion arose. There were few, if any, precedents. There was no man to tell them how or what to do, to map their campaign with statesmanlike strategy. That is why they did so well. They left the strategy to the Holy Spirit and busied themselves in doing his bidding.

For instance, Peter may have known the significance of what he was doing when he carried the gospel into the home of Cornelius, but I doubt it. It was not his strategy but God's that threw open the door of the gospel to the Gentiles. Left to themselves, the apostles very likely would

The Supply of the Spirit

have devoted their efforts like many today to "bringing in the kingdom" at Jerusalem where they were.

Paul is another example. A great deal has been said of his missionary statesmanship. But the strategy of his missionary journeys was not any more the product of his own mind than was the gospel which he preached. He distinctly says that he went up to the Jerusalem conference "by revelation" (Gal. 2:2). All his ministry bears the stamp of the Spirit's peculiar guidance. He was forbidden of the Holy Spirit to speak the word in Asia, and when his party tried to go into Bithynia "the Spirit of Jesus suffered them not" (Acts 16:6-7). It is easy for us in the light of subsequent events to see the wisdom of his crossing westward into Europe, but here again I doubt that he himself knew the full meaning of that eventful Macedonian call. The strategy was not his but God's. And the fruit of his labors revealed the wisdom of the Spirit at every turn, for Spirit-led service is not marred by folly and failure.

One of the most refreshing examples, however, of the way in which the Spirit will direct our service is found in Acts 8:29. "And the Spirit said unto Philip, Go near and join thyself to this chariot." Traveling from Samaria in the north, Philip came finally to the great highway running west from ancient Babylon through Jerusalem and on south to Egypt. It was a great and busy thoroughfare through the desert. His instructions to leave the revival in Samaria had been given him specifically by an angel of the Lord. He was there; what next? Imagine him standing by the wayside in the perplexity which all of us would feel in a like situation. But the still small voice of the Spirit within gave him certainty: "Go near, and join thyself to this chariot." *"This* chariot"—never, I think, was the demonstrative pronoun more comforting. Of all the people traveling that ancient highway, the passenger in "this" chariot alone had the prepared heart. Thus, God arranged the contact. It was in the wise design of the sovereign Spirit that the seeking sinner and the seeking Saviour should meet, as Philip opened his mouth and "preached unto him Jesus" (Acts 8:35).

This specific guidance is for all of God's children on the highway of service. The Spirit of God will direct our lives into the most helpful contacts if we let him. There are ten thousand things to be done. All of them are good, but God does not expect us to do them all. Effective service comes when the Holy Spirit puts us in touch with the need we best can fill, the particular task he has himself assigned to us.

The life of Jesus is revealing when studied from this angle. Even he did not do it all. He was thronged by the multitudes and pressed by many calls. His days were full but not crowded. Nor was he pushed around by circumstances. "Are there not twelve hours in a day?" said he to those who would hurry him from the scene of danger (John 11:9). It was his way of saying there is time enough for what God wants done. The remarkable poise and serenity which characterized Jesus cannot be understood apart from the fact that he was led of the Spirit to make the right emphases, to do the needful things, and to let the others go. He did not break himself down trying to accomplish everything but found contentment in doing step by step the work assigned him by the Father. And so can we, but *how?*

The secret of successful service is the Spirit's guidance, and the secret of the Spirit's guidance is the trained ear, and training an ear takes time and practice. There is the challenge of a promise in our Lord's oft repeated word to the seven churches of Asia, "He that hath an ear, let him hear what the Spirit saith to the churches" (Rev. 2:7 ff). We may not hear so well at first, but we can learn.

Many years ago my father, then a missionary in China, bought my older brother, Gordon, a violin. There was no one to teach him how to play. But mother, who was quite musical, helped him all she could. She showed him how to tune the violin by striking the notes on the piano. This was a laborious process at first, with repeated sounding of the different tones and subsequent tunings. However, Gordon was gifted in music and learned rapidly. It was not long before the striking of one note was all that was necessary. The other strings were tuned from it by an ear that had become trained to hear.

In this training of the inner ear, love has its part too. A young mother can hear the first cry of her babe upstairs above the other voices in the room. Her hearing has been made acute by love. Nothing sensitizes our faculties of discernment like love. The guidance of the Spirit comes about by constant training on one hand and a heart of love on the other. A sense of his leading finally becomes habitual as one learns his ways. At the great crossroads of service the Spirit of God is our never-failing supply of wisdom directing us into the channels of highest usefulness.

THE POWER

We have seen how the Holy Spirit supplies the motivation and the direction in effectual service. But that is not enough without the power to get things done. That, too, is the gift of the Spirit of God. We are utterly powerless without him. We are living in an atomic age. Physical power has been harnessed on an unprecedented scale. For that reason, our age needs spiritual power as never before. When high explosives are rocking the earth, God does not mean that his servants shall join the fray with pop guns. But that is what we often do—holding the form of godliness but denying the power. I am ashamed to say it, but I believe it is true: the world has never seen a time when so much training and so much organization was matched with so little power.

One of the most pathetic sights I remember from the dark days of the depression was in the Chesapeake and Ohio Railroad yards at Russell, Kentucky, one of the largest of its kind in the country. I had never lost my boyhood thrill at the sight of a mighty engine throbbing with power as it puffed across the country with a long train of cars following, or as it pulled up panting at the depot. It all but broke my heart to see these mighty monarchs of the rails idle, powerless, rusting—a helpless prey to the elements. The organization of machinery was there—but no power! This may well represent the sad plight of church after church—highly organized, equipped with fine and necessary machinery, manned with well-trained crews, but devoid of that power from on high which glorifies Christ in the flow of life which it releases. And what is true of churches is true because of the individuals who compose their membership.

But such is not the purpose of our Lord. He means that we shall have power adequate for the need. His command is still, "Tarry ye in the city until ye be clothed with power from on high" (Luke 24:49), and his promise is still, "Ye shall receive power *when the Holy Spirit is come upon you"* (Acts 1:8). The Holy Spirit alone supplies the power we need for effective witnessing—power for prayer, power for personal work, power for holy and victorious living. Whatever God is expecting of us, he has supplied the power to get it done. If we fail through weakness it is not his fault but our own for refusing to tap the boundless energy he supplies. We have not yet learned "the exceeding greatness of his power to us-ward who believe, according to the working of the strength of his might which he wrought in Christ" (Eph. 1:19–20). What an accumulation of power is made available to us in that text! He has never yet sent one servant upon any mission without providing the power necessary to perform it. His very assignment is the guarantee of strength for the task. It was through the power of the Spirit that Jesus wrought his mighty works. By this power also the apostles of old shook the world with their testimony. The scheme of redemption is a vast undertaking, but in the supply of the Spirit is power to see it through.

The development of air power has taken place so rapidly that we are astonished to think how recent all of it actually is. In 1930 Dr. Claudius Dornier, a German engineer and designer of aircraft, astonished the world with the giant DO-X. During the days when the great ship was under construction, reputable experts predicted that she could never lift herself from the lake into the air. Empty, she weighed thirty-three tons. With her full complement of fuel and sixty-nine passengers, she weighed fifty-two tons. When the day for the test flight came, a large crowd gathered at the water's edge. She taxied to position, and then with a roar from her mighty engines she gathered speed. A streak of foam marked her path as she skimmed along the surface of the lake. When the ship with a load greater than that of a crowded railway car broke free from the clinging spray and soared upward like a bird, a cheer went up from the huge throng. The great engineer who had planned the ship had planned also that there should be sufficient power for its operation. The plan of redemption is a vast undertaking. So is the achievement of a single life of victory in these increasingly difficult days. But the Great Architect who drew the plan and designed the life has provided power more than sufficient for the task. The Holy Spirit himself is the living guarantee of its operation.

In the person of his own Spirit who dwells within the believer God has solved forever the problem of supply. He has given us the Spirit of power and love and wisdom. By his own appointment we are here to serve in a world of need. By his own bounteous provision that service is to be glorious and effective. Everything necessary is instantly available at the moment of need. If we do not find this the case, the time has come to examine our own relationship to him. Sin can cut us off and will if we let it—the sin of ignorance, the sin of omission, the sin of selfishness. Any disobedience or shrinking back on our part chokes off the supply. In the sight of his Holy One of whom we have been thinking, any sin is defilement and must be confessed and forsaken. Only thus can the blood of Christ cleanse our conscience from dead works to serve the living God. When this is done, we may freely say with the apostle Paul, "I am a match for all things through him who keeps pouring his power into me" (Phil. 4:13, author's translation). When we are right with him, no power on earth can cut us off from the effective working of his might.

VI

The Ministry of Conviction

The power of the Holy Spirit in connection with his presentation of the truth of the gospel is of such great importance that it deserves special treatment. This ministry is generally described as that of conviction. The primary application of the term is to his procedure in preparing the sinner for the work of regeneration. The difference, however, between that and his preparation of the saint for the work of sanctification is more a difference of subject than of methods or procedure employed. Conviction is a necessary preliminary in either case. Without it there can be no initial experience of salvation or subsequent growth in grace.

The importance of this ministry of conviction was forcefully called to my attention one day as I stood in a public building in a great city. My eye was attracted to a poster with the promise of a huge reward for "information leading to the arrest and conviction" of a certain fugitive from justice. This promise of reward was also accompanied by a picture and a detailed description of the wanted man. But frankly, the effect of the appeal was more monetary than personal. The sum of money involved was a tremendous amount, and the service rendered to the officers of the law was amazingly small—only a bit of information leading to the arrest and conviction of the criminal at large! It was then that the words, *"and conviction,"* stood out with sudden force. It is one thing to arrest a man; it is quite another thing to convict him, as any officer of the law can tell you. Indeed, as any preacher can tell you!

One skilled in the art of conversation can arrest the attention of his hearers easily enough, but how to make the truth stick so as to win the verdict from them is quite another matter. The servant of God, whether he bears his witness or pleads the cause of Christ, is after conviction. Nothing else satisfies. His is the task of bringing every man, woman, and child that has reached the age of accountability under conviction of sin. The verdict of guilt is not to come from the judgment bar of God. That takes place later, when the dead, the great and small, stand before the great white throne (Rev. 20:12). Nor is the pronouncement of guilt to be returned from the tribunal of public opinion. God has never intended for his servants to lower sinners in the eyes of their neighbors and friends by berating them for their misconduct. The verdict in question must be returned from the court within the heart of the individual himself. He must stand convicted before the bar of his own conscience.

I place this emphasis upon the necessity of conviction because the promise of reward is at this point. Only when a man is convicted of his sin will he—can he—accept Christ. To offer a Saviour to one who has not felt the burden of sin is much like a physician offering his services to a man who has not discovered his hidden malady. Unaware of need, he would only thank the physician for his good will and assure him that if sickness should come he would at that time take up the matter of calling a doctor. This attitude is the most frequent response the soul-winner meets, unless by pressing the claims of Christ prematurely it becomes an attitude of actual resentment.

The blessing that follows when a sinner is brought to realize the extent to which he needs the Saviour is more than a matter of acceptance. His witness also is involved. Genuine conviction of sin gives depth and reality to the Christian experience, and this in turn gives vigor to his testimony. His usefulness as a witness, therefore, will be determined by the nature and degree of his experience. People who do not realize that *from* which they are saved, cannot appreciate that *to* which they are saved. To pass out of death into life is a great experience, but from the nature of the testimony of thousands whose names clutter our church rolls, the transition, if made at all, seems to have been effected while they were asleep. Contrast their testimony with that of the unnamed hero of John 9, the man whose eyes, sightless from birth, Jesus opened. There were many questions upon which he could not speak with assurance, but upon one point he was perfectly clear and convincing. "One thing I know, that, whereas I was blind, now I see" (v. 25). To be effective the Christian witness must carry this ringing note of certitude.

We can ill afford to miss this double reward which inevitably attends real conviction. For lack of it much of our witnessing, Bible teaching, and preaching is ineffective. We mean well; our efforts are sincere; we hold forth the truth. Our plans are well laid; our organizations are complete; and our programs are well executed. Why is it, then, that so few cry out, "Sirs, what must I do to be saved?" (Acts 16:30). The answer is that we have not properly related ourselves to the Holy Spirit in his ministry of conviction. Painful experience teaches us that we must enter into this ministry more fully and more intelligently.

THE AGENT

On the night of his betrayal Jesus comforted his disciples with the promise, "If I go, I will send him [the Comforter] unto you. And he, when he is come, will convict the world in respect of sin, and of righteousness, and of judgment" (John 16:8). "He, when *he* is come." Words cannot be arranged to point out with greater emphasis that the Holy Spirit is God's agent in securing conviction. This means, of course, that there can be no other substitute. Yet many substitutes are tried; so many and so likely do they appear that we shall do well to examine them carefully, lest we make the mistake of depending upon them rather than upon the Spirit of God.

Logic is sometimes used as a substitute. In the natural way of thinking, logic is the most direct and most forceful way of presenting truth. For those who make it a science, it is a well-nigh irresistible weapon. Granted a premise, they move step by step to the inexorable conclusion. Some would-be soul-winners adopt this procedure. They marshal their proof-texts as if they could win their prospect by a scriptural syllogism. They fail to see that conviction is more than a logical presentation of the plan of salvation. In religion, as in other areas, "a man convinced against his will is of the same opinion still." This approach, but from a somewhat different extreme, was represented by a minister whom I once heard speaking on the subject to a class of college students. He defined conviction as, "thinking focused to the point of action." On the surface that statement sounds very well, but in the light of Scripture it simply is not so. It fails to recognize the divine illumination necessary if the thinker is to have the facts upon which he must act. Logic, forceful as it is and desirable as it is, can never substitute for the Spirit of God.

Among those who are gifted in such a manner, there is always the danger of substituting eloquence for the ministry of the Spirit in conviction. Few among us recognize the power of well-chosen words, skilfully used, falling with measured cadence like the waters of a fountain, or throbbing with the rhythm of war drums sounding the call to battle. The man with a facile tongue knows people can be talked into anything. Such a man must bring himself under discipline after the example of the apostle Paul. Sometimes he must forego the use of "persuasive words of wisdom" in order to make room for the "demonstration of the Spirit and of power" so that the faith of his hearers will "not stand in the wisdom of men, but in the power of God" (1 Cor. 2:4–5).

A special word of caution needs to be sounded in reference to the danger of relying upon organization and salesmanship rather than upon the Spirit of God to increase the membership of our churches. This is a peril to which we Americans with our genius for organization are peculiarly susceptible, especially in this day of pressure salesmanship. Winning others to profess faith in Christ is the biggest enterprise in all the world. The undertaking needs the discipline of the best in methods and techniques. We should be businesslike in the task our Lord has committed to us, but we must likewise remember the words of the prophet. "Not by might [organization] nor by power, but by my Spirit, saith Jehovah of hosts" (Zech. 4:6).

Nor will tricks of mass psychology and impressive ritual serve in lieu of the Holy Spirit, even though men often resort to those devices to bring others to contrition. I mention these two together because I believe they are expressions of the same disease—symptoms, though different in appearance, of the same malady. One extreme attacks bobbed hair and the use of lipstick among women along with other more or less questionable practices as a cheap substitute for a sense of sin; the other extreme resorts to robes, ornate ritual, chanting choirs, and muttering organs as a substitute for a sense of God. Both fail to recognize that it is the work of the Holy Spirit by making real the presence of God to accomplish the end they have in view.

Emotionalism, even the fear of death itself, is not a substitute for conviction. I have seen saints who were afraid to die, and I have seen sinners who looked upon death without displaying any fear whatsoever. For a man to say he is not afraid to die does not necessarily mean that he is prepared to die. A chicken or a pig has no fear of death. Were such a man to know all the facts in connection with death, his state of mind would be entirely otherwise, and only the Spirit of God can reveal these facts.

I have named these substitutes, and there are many others, to which men resort rather than relying upon God's Spirit, but I must not give the impression that these things are wrong, or even useless. Who would forbid logic and eloquence in pleading the cause of Christ, or who would disparage the orderliness and beauty of an hour of worship devoted under the Spirit's guidance, or the effectiveness and discipline of the most businesslike techniques in the matter of winning others to Christ? It is only when these are allowed to substitute for the work of the Holy Spirit that one can find fault with them. The problem is one of emphasis. Whenever we depend upon the means rather than the agent, confusion is the inevitable result.

We can brook no substitute for the Holy Spirit in this work of conviction. He is the divinely appointed agent. The New Testament affords no clearer illustration of the effectiveness of his agency than in the order of events immediately before and upon the day of Pentecost.

John relates how that in the evening of the day upon which the Lord Jesus was raised from the dead, "when the doors were shut where the disciples were, for fear of the Jews, Jesus came and stood in the midst, and saith unto them, Peace be unto you" (John 20:19). But Thomas, one of the twelve, was not with them at the time. When they told him later that they had seen the Lord, Thomas remained unconvinced. We have the picture of ten men, companions of his for three years, whose word he had never had occasion to doubt, combining their efforts, each bearing his testimony, and all to no avail. The classic reply of this honest doubter was, "Except I shall see in his hands the print of the nails, and put my finger into the print of the nails, and put my hands into his side, I will not believe" (John 20:25). The evidence of all of them together was not sufficient to carry conviction.

A few weeks later, however, we see these same men, Thomas now among them, standing in the midst of a great concourse of people who had come together out of sheer curiosity, but who lingered in amazement at the things which they saw and heard. As this small group testified that God had raised from the dead the Man of Nazareth whom they had crucified and slain, more than three thousand of them were convinced. By act and attitude they made it plain that the witnesses had carried their point. Note the contrasting pictures: ten men uniting their efforts to convince one of their number that Jesus had been raised from the dead; one hundred and twenty convincing three thousand and more that God had raised from the dead and made both Lord and Christ the man whom they had crucified. The difference cannot be explained except by the fact that between the two incidents the Holy Spirit had come.

This preparation in the heart of a sinner, without which there can be neither repentance nor faith, is a supernatural experience. We are inclined to think that it is our part to convince an unsaved man of his need and the Holy Spirit's part to regenerate him. Actually the Holy Spirit does both. It requires as much the "power from on high" for the miracle of conviction as it does for the miracle of regeneration. In our desire to enjoy the fruits of this ministry we must see to it that the Holy Spirit comes into his own.

THE MEANS

The words of Jesus in John 16:8 indicate beyond question that the third person of the Trinity is the agent of conviction; they tell us, however, little about *how* he convicts the heart of an unregenerated person. That, too, we must know in order that we may work intelligently with him.

The most illuminating passage that I have found in the

Bible on the Spirit's mode of procedure as he convicts men and women is Ephesians 5:11, 13. "And have no fellowship with the unfruitful works of darkness, but rather even reprove them. . . . But all things when they are reproved are made manifest by the light; for everything that is made manifest is light." As the margin of the ASV shows, the word here translated "reprove" is the same word as that translated in John 16:8 "convict." The Holy Spirit works through the believer to bring conviction, and he obtains the desired effect by his use of light. In this light, or divine illumination, the sinner comes to see himself in relation to the cardinal points on God's spiritual compass, as we are told in John 16:8–11.

But light is a strange thing, even physical light which forms such a fitting analogy to the spiritual illumination we are discussing. For example, unless one is looking directly towards the light, he does not see it at all except by reflection. On a clear dark night one may stand by a powerful searchlight and, because he cannot see the source of the light, hardly be aware of it at all. Only as dust particles in the atmosphere, moths, or other creatures of the night reflect its rays to him will he recognize the shaft of light which would otherwise lose itself in the illimitable sky above.

This truth was dramatically brought home to me many years ago when I was driving a Model T Ford automobile one night down the steep slopes of the Saluda mountains in South Carolina. It was in the days before roads were well graded and curves along the mountainside carefully indicated by railings painted white. On a particularly steep incline, coming suddenly to a sharp turn, I found myself almost in complete darkness. Thinking that my lights had blown I slammed on my brakes and stopped to consider the emergency. I soon found, however, that my lights were burning as brightly as ever, but facing off from the mountainside there was nothing to reflect their light so that it could be seen by me.

In the days since, this incident has become a parable to me of the sinner's condition. Because his back is to God, he is facing away from the light. To one in this position the light will do no good until it is reflected by others who are themselves in the light. In a very real way the light by which the sinner finds his way is a reflected light, and, for this reason, the conduct and attitude of believers is of utmost importance in convicting an unregenerate person.

The first light that the sinner sees is that which is reflected by someone who is walking in the light. God's light which shines through eternity must be focused by human experience in time and place. It is the believer's privilege to supply this ministry. No one else is in a position to do so. The blessedness of salvation can become manifest only through him. He alone knows the happiness of one whose sins are forgiven, the joy of fellowship with the risen Lord, the peace that passeth understanding, the elation of one who sees all things working together for good. To observe that which others have is to feel most keenly our own lack. Discontent can always be traced to this source, and the "divine discontent" of which we are speaking operates on this same principle. The very best way, therefore, to make a man feel his need of the Saviour is to show him what that Saviour means to us. In our desire to win others to Christ we must remember that the sinner chooses his way in the light which we shed upon his path.

There is an interesting illustration of this truth in

Corinthians 14. This is Paul's famous chapter on worship. Against the background of confusion in worship as the Corinthian church practiced it, he presents the picture of worship as it ought to be, prophets speaking in orderly fashion and the rest discerning (v. 29). Then he describes the effect on the unsaved who might also be present. "But if all prophesy, and there come in one unbelieving or unlearned, he is reproved [the same word, *convicted*] by all, he is judged by all; the secrets of his heart are made manifest; and so he will fall down on his face and worship God, declaring that God is among you indeed." (vv. 24–25).

Here we find three important things: the believer's part in the ministry of conviction, the effect in the heart of the sinner himself, and the end result of open confession to the power of God's presence. The desired result is obtained as believers relate themselves properly to the light of the gospel which is, of course, Jesus. Failure to obtain conviction when we preach or teach the Word can be, therefore, and often is more the fault of the saved than of the unsaved. As long as the Corinthian Christians regarded the privilege of worship as an opportunity to display their own gifts, they were absorbing light rather than reflecting it. Under such circumstances conviction would be difficult indeed, if not impossible. The attitude of the believer himself toward the Word has everything to do with creating the atmosphere in which others may find Christ.

I have dealt at some length with the analogy between physical and spiritual light in this matter of conviction. There is also an instructive parallel in yet another realm. We sometimes speak of light in an intellectual and moral sense, and here again, "all things, when they are convicted are made manifest by the light."

For example, consider how a prosecuting attorney obtains conviction. Some years ago I looked in upon a trial which attracted widespread attention because of the social prominence of the defendant. A dentist was accused of stealing gold in considerable quantity from a dental laboratory. I edged my way into the crowded courtroom just at the time when the janitor of the building where the theft had occurred was in the witness chair. The man was obviously little skilled in speaking before others, but his sincerity was evident to everyone in the room. His answers to the solicitor's questions were direct and spoken with an earnestness that impressed all who heard him that he was telling the truth. Every word in his testimony incriminated the defendant. The solicitor won his case, but the thing to note is that he obtained his conviction by the use of light, light thrown on the case by the evidence of witnesses who testified of the things which they had seen and heard.

Now the Holy Spirit goes about his ministry of convicting the world in much the same fashion. He must have the witness of those who have experienced God's truth as it is in Jesus Christ. Their testimony throws light on the sinner's way. The evidence which they bring searches him out. In the light of their experience he finds himself undone and in need of the Saviour. For example, it was not Peter's sermon alone that the Spirit used to bring conviction at Pentecost. Conviction began when the amazed multitude, gathered from many different lands, heard the simple Galileans speaking in their tongues the mighty works of God. All that Peter did was to sum up the evidence which his fellow disciples had presented. Under similar conditions any man can preach with convicting power.

There is another way in which conviction is obtained in our courts besides through the evidence brought by witnesses. Oftentimes a criminal case "breaks" through confession on the part of someone involved in the crime. Indeed, results come more readily through this method than through any other. Generally speaking, Christians seem slow to realize the close connection between bearing witness and making confession. We are especially slow to use the advantage which is ours in confession. It is much easier to get people to give their testimony for Jesus than it is to get them to confess their sins and put them away in an up-to-the-minute experience of his grace. Yet when church members confess their sins, sinners on the outside are invariably moved to repentance also.

Pride accounts in great part for our reticence in making confession. There is also misunderstanding. It is hard for those of us in the church to realize our complicity in the sins of the world outside, but until we do there is little that we can say that will affect the situation. There are not two versions of the sin question. It is all one problem, and until the children of God are willing to have done with it, we cannot expect the world to be concerned about it. We must remember that there have been revivals without preachers and without singers and without many accepted techniques and procedures, but there have never been revivals where God's people have not confessed and renounced their guilty partnership with the world which crucified their Lord.

This, as I understand it, is the way in which the Holy Spirit convicts the unregenerate. He does it by throwing the light of the Word or, rather, the Light of the world upon the sinner. He presents God's truth through the irresistible evidence of men and women who have experienced it—once lost like himself, but now saved by the grace of God. By divine illumination the unregenerate person understands where he is and what he is—what sin is, and righteousness, and judgment. In this experience he discovers himself, and—better than that, but not apart from that—he discovers Jesus the Saviour.

THE EFFECT

Thus far we have considered the Holy Spirit as the divine agent in conviction and have thought together upon his procedure in bringing the sinner to a realization of his lost condition before God. It remains for us now to give attention to the effect of his ministry, to the results obtained by it.

Our primary concern will not be with the manifestation of that state of mind which we call conviction. Suffice it to say there are many evidences by which the trained eye can detect the hand of the Spirit in preparing the sinner to meet the Saviour. Conviction may come suddenly and dramatically, as it did to the Philippian jailer; or it may come quietly, as in the case of Lydia, "whose heart the Lord opened to give heed unto the things which were spoken by Paul" (Acts 16:14). Sometimes a furious outburst of hostility toward Christ and toward all who bear his name is the sure evidence that the winged truth of God, like an arrow, has penetrated the armor of indifference to pierce the heart. The words of Jesus indicated as much when he said to Saul of Tarsus, "It is hard for thee to kick against the goad" (Acts 26:14).

However conviction comes, and whatever its form of expression, the one end towards which this experience leads is repentance and faith with their fruit of confession. But true conviction may fall short of this goal. A man may harden his heart to the truth. To do so only makes his transgressions more wilful. It exposes him to the awful danger against which God warns those who sin wilfully after they have received the knowledge of the truth (Heb. 10:26; Heb. 6:4–5).

Our primary concern, rather, will be with those truths, or that Truth, of which the convicted man becomes aware in the light which the Spirit of God has thrown upon his way. Our inquiry takes us back again to John 16:8–10: "And he, when he is come, will convict the world in respect of sin, and of righteousness, and of judgment." Here are the cardinal points of God's spiritual compass. Here the lost man, confused and all turned about in his mind, may get his bearings. Here the lost is found, not because others, even God, have located him, but because he finds himself on the map of the spiritual universe and can begin to chart his course accordingly. For the sake of others, and for our own sake, it will be well for us to check our bearings with him.

The convicted man discovers himself in reference to sin. "Of sin, *because they believe not on me,*" said Jesus. He learns that there is a difference between sin and sins far deeper in meaning than the difference between the singular and plural form of a word. He discovers that the sin of unbelief lies at the root of his trouble and that the various "sins" of which he has been aware all along are only the fruitage of this basic unbelief. The fruit now is of lesser importance to him than the tree that bears it.

Parliamentary law supplies a most instructive analogy to the position in which the world finds itself in reference to the claims of the gospel. The question before the "house" is not, Is there a God? The evidences that there is a God are so numerous as to impugn the right of a man who denies them to sit in a deliberative body at all. "Only the fool [the unreasoning man] hath said in his heart, There is no God" (Psalm 14:1).

Rather, the question is, What kind of God is there? It was stated long ago by none other than Jesus himself, who said, "What think ye of the Christ, *whose Son* is he?" (Matt. 22:42). Is Jesus God's Son? Is God *that kind of God?* This question takes precedence above all others. For the sinner, debate upon anything else is out of order because that is the only question he is in a position to do something about. Other matters will come up in due order after that issue is settled, but until then the question posed to the sinner by the great Parliamentarian is ever and only, "What then shall I do with Jesus who is called the Christ?" (Matt. 27:22).

All the evidence of Scripture and experience is marshaled by the Holy Spirit to convince the world that "God gave unto us eternal life, and this life is in his Son" (1 John 5:11). As I understand the verses immediately preceding this quotation, there are three lines of evidence which converge upon this one point: the direct witness of the Spirit himself; the "water," or the testimony of Scripture; and the "blood," or redemption as it has found expression in human experience. A man who weighs this evidence finds himself of necessity faced with the alternatives of accepting Jesus Christ as his Saviour or of making God a liar by denying the witness God has borne to that effect (v. 10).

God's quarrel with man, therefore, is not how many

times he may have cursed, how many robberies, how many acts of adultery, how many murders he may have committed. God probes past these sins, distressing as they are, to the root of the trouble. Did he accept Jesus Christ as his Saviour? If so, the problem of sins is cared for in that act; if not, he has wilfully turned from light to darkness and brought upon himself the inevitable judgment incurred by such a choice. It is the work of the Holy Spirit in conviction to keep this issue which lies at the very heart of the sin question squarely before the world.

Another cardinal point on God's compass is: "of *righteousness*, because I go unto the Father, and ye behold me no more" (John 16:10). The world is as much confused about righteousness as it is about sin. The natural man knows only that righteousness which is related to the moral law, the righteousness which he feels to be his own because he has earned it—which, nevertheless, seems always to need bolstering by his professions and continued "good works." The regenerated man, on the other hand, is concerned only for the righteousness which is related to Jesus Christ, a redemptive righteousness coming from God, given, not earned, finding effect in human experience through faith in Jesus Christ, and returning again in praise to God.

I am not sure that I understand the words of our Lord when he said, "because I go unto the Father, and ye behold me no more" (John 16:10). Apparently they refer to his ascension and to the fact that his righteousness thenceforth could find corporate and manifest expression only through those in whom he was to dwell by faith. This much seems certain: The contention of the Holy Spirit is that righteousness must always be understood in its relation to

Jesus. The righteousness of the scribes and Pharisees (Mark 5:30) stood condemned because it found no room for him. That kind of righteousness, because it stems from the energy of the flesh, because it serves only to inflate the ego, and because it crowds out Jesus, stands condemned in the white light of his ascension.

Therefore, when I hear someone compare himself favorably with the hypocrite in the church, or with the lamentably low standard of conduct prevailing among profession Christians in general, I know I am listening to a man who has not come under the conviction of the Spirit. If such a man undertakes to gain entrance into the kingdom of heaven by virtue of his own righteousness, how good must he be? As good as the apostate church member, or the "average" Christian? He must be so good that when he dies, death, having no claim against him, must release him—even his dead body—in which he shall ascend as by a heavenly law of gravity to seat himself at the right hand of the Majesty on high. No one has a righteousness like this except the holy and righteous One to whom as Saviour the Spirit of God unfailingly directs the attention of man in his morally bankrupt and spiritually insolvent state.

God names a third and final point by which the sinner, once he has seen it, may find his bearings: "of *judgment, because the prince of this world hath been judged*" (John 16:11). The sinner must find himself not only in relation to Christ but also in relation to Satan and the world system of which he is the prince. The choice before him involves two dominions. Will he remain a child of the present order and continue under the dominion of the "prince of the powers of the air, of the spirit that now worketh in the sons of disobedience" (Eph. 2:2), or will he transfer his allegiance to Jesus the Son of God?

There is a cosmic aspect to the cross of Jesus of which one is totally unaware until the Spirit of God makes it plain to him. There the Saviour died not only that he might bear in his body our sins upon the tree, and not only that he might impart the effect of his death to us as sinners, but also that he might deliver us from Satan into whose authority we had fallen because of our sin. In a statement which unmistakably refers to his cross Jesus said, "Now is the judgment of this world; now shall the prince of this world be cast out" (John 12:31). In other words, his death was to be the complete overthrow, the final and utter undoing of Satan.

A passage in Colossians 2:14, as might be expected from the nature of that letter, emphasizes most clearly the cosmic nature of the cross as it describes most vividly the extent of the victory which Christ won there. We are told how the commands which we had broken, the handwriting in ordinances against us, which was contrary to us, were forever taken out of the way and nailed to the cross. We are told also how in doing this, the man Christ Jesus, laden with the sins of the human race, set upon by the combined forces of hell, divested himself forever of the rulers and powers arrayed against him and made a public spectacle of their defeat by triumphing over them in the cross.

There, in the unfolding drama of redemption the battle was won. There the devil and all the minions of hell, the "world-rulers of this darkness" went down in utter and everlasting defeat.

To the sinner, therefore, facing in the gospel the choice between these two dominions, the Holy Spirit makes it perfectly clear that to align oneself with Satan is to choose a portion in his defeat. To continue in his service is to invest time, energy, and substance in an order that is doomed. Judgment is not pending; it is pronounced. "The prince of this world *hath been judged.*" When I hear a man who is not a Christian express the hope that he will not be lost, I take it as a token that he has never really experienced conviction. If he had, he would see himself as part and parcel of a doomed order, condemned already to the lake of fire reserved for the devil and his angels.

Through the experience of conviction the Holy Spirit sees to it that the Christian becomes ready to enter the kingdom of God. The tragedy that follows because we do not rightly relate ourselves to this ministry is not only that so few are prepared to repent of their sins and believe in Jesus as their Saviour, but that so many who profess to do both are still at a loss as to what it is all about. Their half-hearted testimony and their aimless wandering only add to the confusion at a time when vigor and clarity in the gospel witness are needed as never before.

A booklet which fell into my hands some years ago has helped me relate the ministry of conviction to the other good things which God has in store for his people. The divine order seems to be Light—conviction—confession —cleansing—and Life. We who seek the blessings of revival will do well to tarry at the point where in presenting the Light the Holy Spirit brings conviction—the reward is there.

VII

Making Jesus Lord

Now concerning spiritual gifts, brethren, I would not have you ignorant. Ye know that when ye were Gentiles ye were led away unto those dumb idols, howsoever ye might be led. Wherefore I make known unto you, that no man speaking in the Spirit of God saith, Jesus is anathema; and no man can say, Jesus is Lord, but in the Holy Spirit.

1 Corinthians 12:1–3

The great concern of the Holy Spirit is to make Jesus Lord, and rightly so, since the most important thing in any life is its center of authority. In this sphere of growing activity which we call life, filled with measureless possibilities for time and eternity, the paramount question is one of lordship. What power shall exercise dominion over it? In the final analysis there are but two powers contending for the mastery: that of Satan, who would have one say, "Jesus is anathema," and that of the Holy Spirit, who would have one say, "Jesus is Lord." Man must accept one dominion or the other. The battle of the soul is joined at this point.

It is interesting to note how this concern of the Holy

Spirit over Christ's lordship of life is phrased: "No man *can* say, Jesus is Lord, *but in the Holy Spirit.*" Of course, there is a way in which one may call him Lord as a matter of lip service only. Jesus probes deep into the actual dominion of the life when he asks, "Why call ye me Lord, Lord, and do not the things which I say?" (Luke 6:46). To call him Lord is one thing; to have him so is quite another.

It has been said, "Jesus must be Lord of all or he will not be Lord at all." This is a neat phrase and has truth in it, but deep in my soul I question it as an unqualified statement of fact. On the threshold of my ministry God led me into a crisis of consecration. As a young man without the responsibilities that so early and so often seem to tie us to given situations, I said the "irrevocable yes" to the Lord Jesus.

That commitment to him as the supreme authority in my life was as genuine and as definite as any experience I have had. Yet there have been few times that I have felt his lordship over me to be complete. As I advanced spiritually, the frontiers of the inner realm continually rolled back to disclose new territory that had to be claimed and conquered. Uprisings and revolts would come unexpectedly in areas I thought had been brought into subjugation. Stubborn pockets of resistance still remained. In the hidden realm of desire the mastery of Jesus was not absolute, and there was then, as there is now, the problem of wayward thoughts and selfish motives. Jesus was my Lord, but his dominion was not complete, and I knew it.

My experience is not different from that of many others. So much was said to me as a young man about consecration that when I finally came to the point of surrender, I was disappointed to find that consecration was not enough.

That disappointment continued until the refreshing revelation dawned upon me that the Holy Spirit was God's answer to my need. With infinite relief I learned that it was his work to make Jesus Lord. "No man can say, Jesus is Lord, [and be satisfied in the actuality of that fact] but in the Holy Spirit." One cannot make him Lord unaided.

When the Spirit brings a man to surrender to Jesus, he next becomes the occupying power to bring about Christ's actual enthronement within. Thus, the whole work of the Holy Spirit centers in Christ, and the progress of his work in any life may be measured by the degree to which Jesus is actually Lord. When a man is filled with the Spirit, Jesus is Lord; and when Jesus is Lord, a man is filled with the Holy Spirit. The expressions are interchangeable. I say this because there are some who are so taken with being "filled with the Spirit" that they have all but forgotten the lordship of Jesus.

My approach, therefore, to Christ's mastery of the human personality is positive. There is a negative aspect with which we dealt in Chapter II. The dominion of Satan through sin must be renounced. The conflict between self-will and God's will is sharp, and the surrender must be complete. I do not minimize this, but I do say "surrender" is not enough. There are multiplied thousands of people, earnest, well-meaning children of God, who have "surrendered," and yet there has been little manifestation of the victory that comes when Jesus is actually reigning as Lord. The plain truth is they have all but surrendered themselves out of the picture entirely!

Some years ago when the summer slump had laid its paralyzing hand upon the evening attendance at our church, and our young people's activities were such in name only, I made my rounds as pastor, looking in on the various groups which were then in session. Many were absent, but the faithful few were going through the form, at least. With a heavy heart I surveyed the melancholy wreckage created by an almost wholesale exodus of pleasure seekers. From one assembly, however, I heard signs of life. Peeping in the door, I saw four Juniors sitting forlornly with their leader, who was at the piano. The hymn they were singing with abject resignation was, "Have Thine own way, Lord, have Thine own way!" My sense of humor saved me, and as I tiptoed away I thought, How many times amid equally dismal failures are we adults content to go on singing our surrender to the Lord!

The reason for this state of affairs is even more distressing than the results which shame us. Our people are following the only leadership they have; they are responding to almost the only kind of preaching they get. All they hear are appeals to consecration, and virtually the only proposals made are to dedication or the much-loved proposition of "rededication." They are led to think that if they only surrender, Jesus will take over automatically. Experience, however, proves that such is not the case. One cannot so blithely by-pass the ministry of the Spirit. "No man can say, Jesus is Lord, but in the Holy Spirit."

THE REALM WITHIN

There is a realm within over which Jesus is definitely to be enthroned as Lord and Master. God names that realm when he says, "Sanctify *in your hearts* Christ as Lord" (1 Peter 3:15). He means that Jesus must be upon the throne of our personality. The Holy Spirit would make Jesus Lord in our heart-life—in our affection and desires.

in our thoughts and imaginations, in our intents and purposes. This is the realm which someone has aptly described as "The Empire of the Soul."

The first time I heard that phrase was from the lips of a speaker who often indulged in flights of oratory. It fell pleasingly upon my ear, and I received it as only an embellishment of speech. But I have had occasion many times since to reflect upon its tremendous significance. However obscure we may seem to ourselves or others, each is a king over a turbulent realm within, whose frontiers range further than he has ever explored and whose affairs of court are far more complex than he has ever imagined. This is the kingdom which each of us must bring under the sway of the Lord Jesus. Unless we do, sin reigns, and we are king in name only.

Our desires are to become sanctified by his lordship. All our rich and varied emotions are to be refined by the fires of his love so that our testimony may have warmth and color and charm. Under his mastery our thoughts and imaginations are to be lifted from the sordid things of a sensual life and cleansed and strengthened to take hold upon the marvelous provisions of his love—those things "which eye saw not, and ear heard not, and which entered not into the heart of man, whatsoever things God prepared for them that love him" (1 Cor. 2:9). Our wills are to be liberated from the bonds of selfishness and strengthened to achieve with a new daring the wondrous purposes of God. Such an interpretation of his lordship is utterly impossible of realization apart from the Holy Spirit, who enters as the occupying power to see that all of this and more is actually brought about.

The acceptance of Jesus as Lord assures the unification

of personality. Till then, we are a divided house—self-will
and God's will alternately in command. Quietness comes
when the central authority of Christ has been established.
This crisis of consecration, however, is but the point of
inception from which the Holy Spirit must continue
with our ready co-operation to make his lordship actual
throughout the whole of our being. He reveals one by one
the hidden pockets of resistance and makes us skilful in the
use of those weapons which are "mighty before God to the
casting down of strongholds; casting down imaginations,
and every high thing that is exalted against the knowledge
of God, and bringing every thought into captivity, to the
obedience of Christ" (2 Cor. 10:4–5). All this he does, not
through surrender alone, but through our own intelligent
and active co-operation.

It is important to recognize that the state of being "filled
with the Spirit" is not one of passivity. Christ does not
reign over our personality by virtue of our abdication; he
reigns because we actively choose him as Lord through our
glad obedience. The self-denial upon which he insists
(Luke 9:23) is not the destruction of our individuality but
rather its preservation and fulfilment. His reign is the
guarantee of our own highest self-realization. Such realization is a part of our original heritage as creatures made in
God's image. "And God created man in his own image, in
the image of God created he him; male and female created
he them: and God blessed them, and God said unto them
. . . *subdue . . . and have dominion*" (Gen. 1:27–28).
Of course, this dominion was then, as it is now, circum-
scribed by limitations of God's own choosing. The point
is that it is a natural part of man's heritage to enjoy it.
It was given to man before the accident of sin befell the

human race. In the kingdom of God the exercise of this God-given attribute of human nature is not taken away but enhanced through the riches of grace.

God intends for men to exercise this dominion in the realm within. He sets great store by it as the following Scriptures will show. "He that is slow to anger is better than the mighty; and he that ruleth his spirit, than he that taketh a city" (Prov. 16:32). "Let not your heart be troubled," said Jesus (John 14:1). It is the fact that he is on the throne of our hearts that keeps them in peace, but we have a responsibility too. We do the "letting." The faith that puts him in charge and keeps him there is ours.

In 1 Corinthians 14:1 the gift of prophecy is described as one to be greatly desired, and is manifestly of the Spirit's own working. Yet even in the exercise of this ministry, "the spirits of the prophets are *subject to the prophets* for God is not a God of confusion, but of peace" (1 Cor. 14:32–33). "The fruit of the Spirit is . . . self-control" (Gal. 5:22–23). All of these Scriptures show that in making Jesus Lord, the Holy Spirit does not ignore man's responsibility. Man becomes no automaton. God's control of a life is brought about through self-control redeemed and restored by grace. Thus, Jesus reigns in the heart, not by setting aside our will, still less by imposing his upon us, but by working in us "both to will and to do of his good pleasure" (Phil. 2:13, KJV; cf. Heb. 13:21).

How God can be sovereign and yet remain free has through the centuries posed a problem to philosophers and theologians. The Scriptures teach both truths, but we have difficulty in reconciling them because they seem mutually contradictory. Perhaps our difficulty comes very largely because we insist on measuring God by our own yardstick.

"Thou thoughtest that I was altogether such a one as thyself: but I will reprove thee" (Psalm 50:21).

The unspiritual man thinks of God's will as he does his own. Because of a selfish bias in his nature, he thinks of the fulfilment of God's will in terms of the expense of others instead of in terms of their highest self-realization. Sin has so warped his outlook that he cannot realize that God's will is the highest good of all, or, to state it another way, that the noblest exercise of man's free choice is also the fulfilment of God's free choice for him. The Holy Spirit dwelling in the believer dignifies the human will by making it want to do God's pleasure. Instead of being fettered, therefore, by the divine indwelling, a man is freed by it. Therein he finds his highest liberty—"Where the Spirit of the Lord is, there is liberty" (2 Cor. 3:17). The triumph of grace is this freedom to enjoy the dominion which was our heritage from the beginning.[1]

[1] One of the finest statements I have read on the whole subject of God's sovereignty and human freedom is in a paragraph from a sermon by Dr. William Temple, at that time Archbishop of York. "And they (irreligious men) argue thus because, having little or no inward experience of religion, they conceive the action of the infinite will of God upon our finite wills to be identical with the action of one man's will upon another's. Even in logic that error is easily refuted. But the lesson of history is very clear. Those men to whom such doctrines as Predestination, Irresistible Grace, the Sovereign Decrees of God, are matters not of speculation but of experience, are precisely those who exhibit the most astonishing energy, conceiving enterprises and performing feats of perseverance and endurance that put to shame the advocates of the view that by independent human volition, we are to discharge a responsibility which is itself felt as an almost crushing burden. St. Paul and St. Augustine, Luther, Calvin, and John Knox, are not names suggestive of quietism; their sense that they were clay in a potter's hands did not lead them to watch with an interested detachment what the potter would make of them or of others; it inspired them to superhuman exertions; and it did this because they knew that the clay which the Potter moulds is not some inert mass of lifeless human qualities, but is the living will of men." C. W. Hale Amos, *The Church and the World* (London: Marshall, Morgan and Scott, Ltd.), p. 161.

However, man's freedom within the sovereignty of God's grace must be carried a step further. We have spoken of the highest expression of man's will in terms of his submission to God. We must now recognize the fact that the noblest function of the will is not surrender but assertion. The strength of the will is seen like that of the tree—not in its bowing to the storm but in its remaining upright after the fury is passed.

A study of the use of the imperative mode in the book of Acts is most rewarding in this connection. Mode is a word the grammarians use to describe the manner in which a thing is said. The imperative mode is that in which commands are given. In it one can hear the ring of authority as the *imperator* speaks. In instance after instance the Spirit-filled followers of Jesus used this mode as they seized the initiative and issued their commands.

Peter's sermon at Pentecost begins and ends with the imperative. The next two chapters hang on his command to the cripple at the Gate Beautiful, "In the name of Jesus Christ of Nazareth, *walk*" (Acts 3:6). Their triumphant progress on through the unfolding pages of Acts is the romance of divine-human initiative. Strike out the use of the imperative in this book and you have mutilated it almost beyond recognition. What the story of the early disciples would be like without their use of the imperative one can only imagine from the reports of some of our own proceedings!

This note of command is the lost chord of Christianity today. We can walk with Peter into the room where the still form of Dorcas lies; after putting all others out, we can kneel with him there, shut in with our dead and with our God; but *we balk at the imperative*. We choke at the words, "Tabitha, arise" (Acts 9:40). And the kingdom of God tarries because we dare not assert a commanding faith. But Christ, when he is truly made Lord, will overcome this paralysis. The Spirit's quickening touch will nerve our initiative and lend the charm of spontaneity to the testimony we bear in Jesus' conquering name.

THE REALM WITHOUT

Thus far our attention has been focused on making Jesus Lord in the turbulent empire of the soul. But there is a realm outside of this in which he must reign also before victory is complete. I refer to the realm of *circumstance*.

Spiritual maturity may be gauged by one's attitude toward the environment which surrounds him. The extent to which a man makes Jesus Lord will determine whether he is victim or victor in that area. I do not mean that this mastery of circumstances is to eventuate in a perfect world order. The perfect order must wait; God is now in the process of perfecting sons and daughters to the glory of his name (Heb. 2:10). But I do mean that the Holy Spirit will enable a man to capture the situation in which he finds himself and capitalize upon it, wresting even from life's darkest moments their tribute to Christ.

The circumstances with which we shall be especially concerned in this study are encountered chiefly as a result of the militant attitude described above. The man of God who takes the initiative is certain to encounter the fiercest opposition of Satan. The militant Christian will find himself continually in situations where Satan tries to defeat him either by temptation or by persecution. In both of these experiences God makes real his "very present" help.

When we are beset by temptation, the Holy Spirit stands

ready to do for us exactly what he did for Jesus when he was tempted. Because this great battle in the wilderness was fought by the Man Jesus, the account of his victory holds special significance for us. We are to win as he won, through the power of the same Spirit.

"And Jesus," we read in Luke 4:1-2, "full of the Holy Spirit, returned from the Jordan, and was led in [by] the Spirit in the wilderness during forty days, being tempted of the devil." Many years ago I penned this statement upon the margin of my Bible by this verse, "A man may be led of the Holy Spirit and tempted of the devil at the same time." It sounds strange, but it is true; and in its strangeness lies a lesson. The Spirit leads the child of God to take the initiative in temptation. There are some things which he led Jesus to fight out with the tempter at the very beginning of his ministry.

If a man waits until the hour of temptation to decide what to do, the battle is virtually lost at the start. It is too late after the devil has set the stage. The secret of a victorious life lies in keeping the initiative. In spiritual warfare as in other areas of conflict, the enemy must be kept off balance by a vigorous offensive. In leading out thus, many a situation is robbed of its potential danger by the aggressiveness of a man on the move for his Lord. For instance, note the example of Jesus, who seized and kept the initiative when he talked with the sinful woman at the well of Samaria (John 4:1-38). Casual conversation with such a character might easily drift in the wrong direction. But Jesus, who spoke the first word, kept the initiative right on to the glorious culmination when he revealed himself to her as the promised Messiah.

As long as one maintains the initiative with Christ he

is safe, but once he yields that initiative to the enemy the results will be tragic indeed. Anything can happen then, as David found out when he took things easy at Jerusalem "at the time when kings go out to battle" (2 Sam. 11:1). The emphasis must be kept on the positive. "Walk by the Spirit, and ye shall not fulfill the lust of the flesh" (Gal. 5:16).

Taking and keeping the initiative in this age-long conflict with evil is really a very simple and practical thing. It has to do with quiet decisions made beforehand, like the one made by a faithful deacon in a rural community. Back in the days of once-a-month preaching, it was the custom of his church to hold business sessions on Saturday afternoon before each preaching Sunday. Although those meetings were poorly attended, this good man always managed to be in his place. Someone asked him how, with his many duties about the farm, he found time to attend with such regularity. By way of reply he said, "I settled that long ago when I first became a Christian. I decided then that the Lord's business was more important than mine, and that when my church met in business session I would be there. I don't have to go all over that each month, I settled it at at the start." He had the right attitude. If church members everywhere would settle the matter of their attendance on that basis instead of fighting a battle each Sunday whether to go or stay, they could use their energies for other battles which they have yet to win, not only in their own lives, but in prayer for others.

There are certain things about the Christian life which we should settle at the very beginning. We should fight these matters out with the tempter on the grounds and at the time of our own choosing and not his. The Holy Spirit will see to this if we are open to his leadership. All that he did for the Man Jesus he stands ready to do for us. He will anticipate the attacks of the adversary and force the issue with him under circumstances advantageous to the Christian. When the onslaught is actually begun, he will quicken some portion of the Word with which to foil the enemy's power. He will teach us how to become skilful in using the "sword of the Spirit" (Eph. 6:17) and all the other weapons in the Christian's arsenal. When he maps the strategy of our warfare, we will come from the field of conflict "more than conquerors."

Under the generalship of the Spirit this power will be with us as it was with the Lord Jesus. He did not come away from his long encounter with the enemy a nervous wreck on the verge of a collapse. Rather, he "returned in the power of the Spirit into Galilee; and a fame went out concerning him through all the region round about" (Luke 4:14). Temptations thus will become an "English Waterloo." [2] "Each victory will help us some other to win," as the hymn says.

The Holy Spirit also stands ready to help in another phase of the Christian warfare, persecution. This is a more advanced form of opposition reserved for those whose progress marks them out to the enemy as conspicuous targets. Persecution may be brought about through agents who can be seen, men and women through whom Satan works, or it may come, as in the case of Job, through no human agency. In the latter case the battle is all the more fierce. This distinction is very significant, although I believe it is rather generally overlooked.

[2] S. D. Gordon, *Quiet Talks About the Tempter* (Edinburgh: Fleming H. Revell Company), p. 21.

Our attitude toward afflictions would be greatly im-
proved if we recognized that the difference between them
and persecution is often only a *difference between agents
seen and unseen*. Both have the same Satanic source, and
both of them have the same Satanic purpose: "give up,
renounce God and die" (Job 2:9). Both offer the same reward to those who patiently endure. There are many
Christians today who would as cheerfully suffer for Jesus'
sake as did the martyrs of old. Yet these same children of
God often lose the joy of Christ's presence in adversity
because they fail to see the same persecutor behind the
scene. The only difference is that now the adversary has
resorted to more subtle methods to hinder their witness.
Regardless of whether the agents through which it comes
are seen or unseen, of this we may be sure, persecution will
come for those who live godly in Christ Jesus (2 Tim. 3:12).

This threat of opposition is very real, though usually
the dread of it is worse than the experience itself. When
Jesus sent forth his disciples as sheep in the midst of wolves,
he gave them this comfort: "But when they deliver you
up, be not anxious how or what ye shall speak; for it shall
be given you in that hour what ye shall speak. For it is not
ye that speak, but the Spirit of your Father that speaketh
in you" (Matt. 10:19). His promise is that the Comforter
will take over in the hour of persecution, if we let him.

That promise has been more than vindicated in the book
of Acts and in the records since. In its realization Peter
slept in utter relaxation the night before he was to have
been executed by Herod (Acts 12:6). His appearance with
John before the Sanhedrin is another triumphant example
of the way the Holy Spirit came to the disciples' rescue
(Acts 4:5–13). Not only did he supply them with a mouth

and wisdom which all their adversaries could not gainsay (Luke 21:15), but he also used the occasion as a sounding board causing the gospel to be heard more effectively and in wider circles than would otherwise have been possible.

The book of Judges also has a message of encouragement for those of us who are inclined to worry about the opposition that is certain to follow an all-out stand for Christ. It gives illuminating insight into the ways of the Spirit among men. We read there of divine enablings when the Spirit of God came mightily upon the heroes of faith. These enablings were sudden outbursts of God's sovereign power, and they were in every case *provoked by the opposition.*

Samson, for example, may not have been a giant among men, marked as God's strong man by bulging muscles and a powerful physique. The secret of his strength lay in God's call and enabling. As he journeyed down to Timnath a young lion roared against him. That was the challenge. "And the Spirit of Jehovah came mightily upon him, and he rent him as he would have rent a kid; and he had nothing in his hand" (Judges 14:6). This experience was his introduction to the way of the Spirit. It is a way we shall do well to learn. We want the awareness of God's presence, especially as we face trouble. But that is not always granted nor is it necessary. What God wants us to accept by faith is that he will be there when the time comes. The roaring of the lion does not frighten the man who is full of the Spirit; it challenges him. Today, as in the time of the Judges, the shout of the enemy is the signal for divine enabling.

Thus, when Jesus is Lord in the realm of circumstance, he is not so much concerned with eliminating the opposition as with capitalizing upon it to make the devices of

the enemy serve his own royal purpose. By his Spirit he
endows the soldier of the cross with the faculty for cashing
in on his afflictions so beautifully described by Words
worth in the "Character of the Happy Warrior."

> Who, doomed to go in company with Pain,
> And Fear, and Bloodshed, miserable train!
> Turns his necessity to glorious gain;
> In face of these doth exercise a power
> Which is our human nature's highest dower;
> Controls them and subdues, transmutes, bereaves
> Of their bad influence, and their good receives.

I wonder, after all, if most of us have not missed the
meaning of our troubles entirely. There is an analogy be
tween them and swimming. Most people like to swim; it
is a thrilling sport. But water is the only element a man
can swim in, and water has its dangers. A man can drown
in it. Many people who would like to swim are afraid of
water. When they try to swim, instead of relaxing and al
lowing the water to bear them up, they get frantic and
wear themselves out trying to swim out of it, not realizing
that the water is the swimmer's friend, not his foe. The
swimmer knows it is not necessary to keep much of his
body out of the water—only his nose and mouth—and that
not all of the time, just now and again for breathing. As
long as he is swimming, water is his element, and he en
joys it. Most people like to live a life of victory. There is a
thrill in that, too. We want victory, continuous victory
but we forget that victory means opposition—continuous
victory, continuous opposition. The way to triumph over
trouble is not to get out of it but to put it to work—ride
it as one rides the waves of the sea. The Holy Spirit has
come to convert our liabilities into assets.

During my seminary days discussion in one of the classes turned to the matter of scholastic degrees, whereon our wise professor found occasion to remark: "After all, young gentlemen, there is only one degree that really counts. It is worth all others put together." Then, pausing to sharpen the interest of the class, he said, "And that is the M.S. degree." Puzzled, the students looked first at him and then at one another. He continued with solemn emphasis, "And M.S. stands for *Master of the Situation*. That degree crowns them all."

I have often thought of the truth in my old professor's remarks. Life is made up of situations, one after another. That man is graduated "Master of the Situation" who, speaking in the Spirit of God, can say, Jesus is Lord.

In every life and under all conditions the great concern of the Holy Spirit is with the lordship of Jesus. The question is the exercise of dominion—God's or Satan's. The battle is joined at this point. There are still those about us spiritually blind, or, as Paul put it, "led away to those dumb idols, however ye might be led." There are others numbered among us who are stifled in the dry rot of empty formalism, dying of boredom without knowing that the battle of the ages surges around them. Yet others are cringing in the face of adversity or fleeing from reality by piously surrendering to Jesus when they should be boldly claiming ground and winning others in his name. The challenge of the Holy Spirit is unmistakably clear. He stands ready if we heed with courageous and intelligent devotion his call to make Jesus Lord both in the turbulent empire of the soul and in the troubled circumstances amid which our lot is cast.

VIII

The Promise of Pentecost

There is a law of mathematics to the effect that things equal to the same thing are equal to each other. If we apply this principle to the interpretation of two passages of Scripture, we shall discover a combined value of richer meaning than that of each taken separately. The two verses are from different accounts of the same teaching of Jesus given by Matthew and Luke. Getting what is good by means of prayer is the particular topic under discussion. According to Matthew, Jesus says, "How much more shall your Father who is in heaven give good things to them that ask him?" (Matt. 7:11). According to Luke, Jesus says, "How much more shall your heavenly Father give *the Holy Spirit* to them that ask him?" (Luke 11:13). Matthew and Luke may be reporting two different occasions, but the underlying truth is the same and the conclusion obvious. Every good thing that God offers the Christian is summed up in the gift of his Holy Spirit. When we have him we have God's best. With him all things else eventuate in due process; without him all things else prove woefully lacking.

The third member of the Godhead is the answer to the Christian's every need. We have seen that as the Divine Executive he comes to make effective *in* us all that Jesus did *for* us. Solving the problem of self by mortifying the deeds of the body, he leads us on into a life of fruit bearing and of joy. He fans into flame the fires of devotion that so often smolder upon the altar of our hearts. His quickening breath transforms our prayer life and vitalizes our reading of the Word. When the going is difficult, the Holy Spirit as the believer's Comforter imparts encouragement and inspiration. He is our never-failing source of supply, the great Enabler, who adequately equips us as servants of God for whatever task is assigned. It is he also who actually makes Jesus Lord and by doing so sets us free to reign as kings over the turbulent empire of the soul.

If these studies together have helped to awaken a longing for the Spirit of God in all his fulness, I am profoundly grateful. In God's order, conviction must always precede appropriation. Our utter need must register itself in thirstiness of soul, for a man's thirst is ever the measure of his drinking from the fountain. If, then, a real thirst has been aroused, it is my prayer that the message in this closing chapter may be used to satisfy that longing "above all that we ask or think according to the power that worketh in us" (Eph. 3:20).

The discussion here will center on Pentecost and the promise made on that memorable occasion when God the Spirit came upon men in a manner never experienced before. Pentecost inaugurated the Christian witness, and nothing short of that which was given then can adequately perpetuate it. The account of the Spirit's coming and

Peter's interpretation of it reveal certain principles which will apply to the end of the age. With this in mind let us examine more particularly the great promise with which Peter closed his message on that significant occasion: "Repent ye, and be baptized every one of you in the name of Jesus Christ unto the remission of your sins; and ye shall receive the gift of the Holy Spirit. For to you is the promise, and to your children, and to all that are afar off, even as many as the Lord our God shall call unto him" (Acts 2:38–39).

Two things are promised: first, the remission of sins; second, the gift of the Holy Spirit. One follows upon the other. All who have dealt faithfully with the sin question through genuine repentance are in a position to claim the gift of the Spirit. It is a part of the same promise.

Now may I get personal? In the light of the circumstances on that memorable day of Pentecost, the gracious outpouring of the Holy Spirit is as much for *you* as it was for the early disciples. Words cannot be plainer. If you do not feel included among those to whom the direct statement was made on that particular day, you must feel the loving embrace of the specific statement, "to all that are afar off, even as many as the Lord our God shall call unto him." It is not a special blessing for a special few in a special age. It is for all who have truly repented and found remission of sins in the blood of the Lamb. Read it again, "To *you* is the promise." The question, therefore, is not whether as a Christian you have a right to the gift of the Spirit, but whether you have claimed that right and availed yourself of this glorious privilege. Have you been filled with the Holy Spirit? Would you like to be? Then let us follow on.

THE PROMISE MADE

The use of the definite article shows that Peter had in mind a very specific promise, and to make it as definite with us as it was with him, let us consider three questions that quite naturally arise before one accepts any promise on face value: who made the promise, what was promised, and why?

Clearly God the Father promised this outpouring of the Holy Spirit. The closing statement of Peter's sermon makes that plain. "Being therefore by the right hand of God exalted, and having *received of the Father* the promise of the Holy Spirit, he hath poured forth this which ye see and hear" (Acts 2:33). Just before his ascension Jesus was even more specific. His parting instruction to his disciples was for them "to wait for the *promise of the Father,* which, said he, ye heard from me" (Acts 1:4). The Father had made it long ago through the prophet Joel (2:28-32). During the centuries since, it had been largely forgotten even by the devout. The Lord Jesus, however, refreshed their minds concerning it. Through the closing days of his earthly ministry he had laid increasing emphasis upon it. His final instruction, as we have seen, was for them to tarry in Jerusalem until its fulfilment. Through the ten days of waiting they thought of little else.

Anyone who has made a note at a bank is familiar with the way a promise can be made and forgotten until in the fullness of time, the due date rolls around. That is the way of promises, whatever the circumstances. Sitting in the drug store many years ago, my little daughter and I were about to order some refreshments. Not realizing that she had been fascinated by a lavish sign advertising a serving of ice cream embellished by all the tasty delights which a modern drug store can provide, I invited her to order what she pleased. "I'll take one of them," she said, pointing at the sign. On the defensive immediately, I replied that a banana split was more of an investment than I thought we ought to make (it was midwinter at the time) and by way of extricating myself from the predicament I said, "Wait till the Fourth of July, when something like that will be more in order." That seemed quite satisfactory with her, and I promptly forgot the incident. But the Fourth of July came in due course, and with it the claim of a little girl who had not forgotten. There was nothing for me to do but to make good the word I had spoken.

Sometimes promises have a way of slipping up on us. The promise of Pentecost was made in the long ago, and now the time had come when those who were first to enjoy its provisions needed to be reminded of it and made ready for the experience. Thus, the Son revived this promise of the Father, and, as it were, endorsed it.

The promise itself has been variously stated. The passage from Joel quoted by Peter reads: "And it shall be in the last days, said God, I will pour forth of my Spirit upon all flesh" (Acts 2:17). Jeremiah's description varies somewhat but in essence the idea is the same: "But this is the covenant that I will make with the house of Israel . . . I will put my law *in their inward parts,* and *in their heart* will I write it; and I will be their God, and they shall be my people" (Jer. 31:33). Paul seems to sum up several versions of the promise in 2 Corinthians 6:16, "Even as God said, *I will dwell in them, and walk in them; and I will be their God, and they shall be my people.*" The clearest and simplest statement of all was made by Jesus in reference to the Comforter: "He abideth with you, and shall be *in* you." (John 14:17).

The thing to notice about all these references is the *inwardness* of the experience they describe. From the beginning man was made to be indwelt. God's plan was to dwell within the believer through his Holy Spirit. In this way, and in this way alone, could the provisions of the new covenant be fulfilled. Those who entered into this covenant with him were to become living temples of God. Jesus regarded his body as God's temple (John 2:21). Paul wrote to the Corinthians, "Know ye not that your body is a temple of the Holy Spirit which is in you?" (1 Cor. 6:19).

No one can ever really understand the human body or appreciate the sublime nature of its capacities until he realizes that it was created to be indwelt by this Holy Spirit. Just as the tabernacle was not complete until it had been filled with the glory-cloud that marked the presence of the Lord God of Hosts, so the human body falls short of its highest destiny until it becomes completely possessed by the Spirit of God.

There is something tremendously satisfying in the realization of this idea. One morning as I drove to my work I saw evidence on a vacant lot at the corner below our home that someone was preparing to build. From day to day I watched the process with great interest. First there was the necessary excavation for the basement and foundation. With astonishing rapidity the concrete was poured and the house began to take shape. It was to be two stories, I noticed, as brick by brick the structure rose. A week later carpenters were putting on the roof. After that the progress seemed slower, but it was evident that workmen were busy inside. Decorators went about their task within, and landscape gardeners were planting shrubbery and beautifying the premises. One day as I saw the windows being cleaned, I thought, It's about finished! But there was still a sense of incompleteness. Something yet was wanting even after the furniture had been installed. And then one night I returned later than usual from my work. The new house on the corner was ablaze with lights. Our neighbors had moved in. Turning into my own driveway that night I experienced a sense of deep satisfaction. The little drama in brick and mortar which I had been watching with such interest was finished. The house had become a home. The purpose of its construction had been achieved —the owner and builder had moved in to occupy.

Thus, the human personality is never complete until God moves in to fill it with the glory of his own presence. A sense of something lacking—whatever you call it, emptiness, vanity, frustration—is the great problem today. The spectre of inadequacy haunts us, and its gloom can only be dispelled by the radiant presence of him who has come to fill us with all the fullness of God. We are so made that we can be satisfied with nothing less. Nor can God. It is the goal toward which he has been working through the ages. Someone has noted that in the days of the Old Testament God was for his people; in the days of the New Testament when Jesus was here in the flesh as our Immanuel, God was with his people; but in these days since Pentecost God has been *in* his people, making his home in them, working in and through them his own purposes of grace.

But why, may we ask, was this blessing only a promise all through the long days from Joel to Peter? The need was certainly urgent from the beginning. The inadequacies created by sin are apparent in the record all along. Why did God meet them with only a promise? The answer to this question requires us to distinguish between the ministry of the Holy Spirit in the old covenant and his ministry in the new. In finding it we shall come to understand why the Spirit would move, for instance, upon a man of such moral standards as Samson while demanding today so much more by way of consecration from those whom he uses.

The eternal Spirit has from the beginning existed coequal with the Father and the Son, but only after the ascension of Jesus could he dwell in the human heart as he does now under the covenant of grace. Until Pentecost had come, the only thing that God could do was to make a promise. With the greatest reverence and yet in all frankness, we must recognize that God made the promise of the Spirit just as many of us make our own promissory notes. We do not have the money at the time, but are sure that when the note comes due we shall be able to arrange its payment. You see, even God himself cannot bestow that which he does not possess—except by promise.

Until Jesus came, God's own quality of life—eternal or "uncreated"[1] life—had never found expression in human nature. God's life had never been translated, so to speak, into human experience. To change the figure, eternal life had not yet been typed for the transfusion so sorely needed by the human race. Since God's quality of life was not suited to be lived out by man, the Spirit could only periodically "come upon" men and pass on, moving them with mighty power in the process. Nowhere in all the universe was there a deathless, victorious, human life perfectly unfolding itself in answer to the requirements of God's own

[1] Mary E. McDonough, *God's Plan of Redemption*.

holy nature which he could impart to man—nowhere until Jesus, the Son of God and the Son of Man, achieved it. Jesus gave the life of God human expression. Through his identification with the human race, and more particularly through his resurrection and ascension, Christ made eternal life suitable for man's appropriation and enjoyment through the Holy Spirit. Now his life becomes ours as truly as the life of the vine becomes that of the branch.

The tremendous significance of the ascension and its connection with Pentecost has been overlooked by many students of the Bible. We must remember that when Jesus ascended, something went to heaven that had never been there before. It was the Man Christ Jesus—the "Man in the Glory." [2] Our Lord carried the priceless trophy of his perfect humanity back to the throne, from whence at Pentecost it was poured out on all flesh through the Holy Spirit. Thus, "when he ascended on high, he led captivity captive and gave gifts unto men" (Eph. 4:8).

Writing of Jesus' invitation given at the feast of the tabernacles (John 7:37–39) Bishop Andrew Murray says, "The Holy Spirit who had come from Christ's exalted humanity to testify in our hearts what Christ had done, was indeed no longer only what he had been in the Old Testament. . . . He came now, first as the Spirit of the glorified Jesus." [3]

Let us examine more carefully this revealing promise, "Now on the last day, the great day of the feast, Jesus stood and cried, saying, If any man thirst, let him come unto me and drink. He that believeth on me, as the scrip-

[2] *Ibid.*
[3] Andrew Murray, *With Christ, in the School of Prayer* (New York: J. H. Sears, Inc.), p. 176.

ture hath said, from within him shall flow rivers of living water. But this spake he of the Spirit, which they that believe on him were to receive; for the Spirit was not yet *given;* because Jesus was not yet glorified" (John 7:37–39).

Notice that the word "given" is in italics, indicating that it was supplied by the editors. It does not occur in the Greek. Try leaving it out: "For the Spirit was not; because Jesus was not yet glorified." Of course, this is not to deny the pre-existence of the Holy Spirit who is from the beginning one with the Father and the Son. I understand it simply to mean that there was no human quality[4] in the divine nature until the Man Jesus took it there by his ascension into God's glory. Once that had been accomplished, and the life stream of the human race had been merged with that of God Himself, rivers of living water could well flow from within. Through the Spirit's indwelling, the Fountain of Life had become established within the believer.

I have gone into much detail concerning the nature of this promise of Pentecost out of a profound conviction that there is a connection between it and the ascension which, for the most part, has been overlooked. Peter unmistakably linked the two together in his memorable sermon by saying: "Being therefore by the right hand of God exalted, and having received of the Father the promise of the Holy Spirit, he hath poured forth this which ye see and hear."

[4] I am reminded here of a sublime passage in "Saul," where Browning passionately voices the yearning of every heart:

" 'Tis the weakness in strength, that I cry for! my flesh, that I seek
   In the Godhead! I seek and I find it. O Saul, it shall be
   A Face like my face that receives thee; a Man like to me,
   Thou shalt love and be loved by, for ever: a Hand like this hand
   Shall throw open the gates of new life to thee! See the Christ stand!"

His next sentence makes it clear that he had the ascension in mind, but we have been slow to grasp the interrelation between the two. This is unfortunate, because without an understanding of the ascension one is hardly in a position to appreciate the outpouring of the Holy Spirit which ushered in this age of grace.

THE PROMISE FULFILLED

The main thing to remember about Pentecost, then, is the fact that the Holy Spirit came exactly as the Father and the Son had promised. One can easily overlook this in the excitement of the occasion.

> O spread the tidings 'round, wherever man is found,
> Wherever human hearts and human woes abound;
> Let ev'ry Christian tongue proclaim the joyful sound:
> The Comforter has come!
>
> F. BOTTOME

A man can be so taken with the spectacular circumstances surrounding an event that he misses its true significance. The magician takes advantage of this human trait to perform his tricks. He diverts attention to one activity or another so that his sleight of hand escapes observation. This does not mean, of course, that God works sleight of hand, but rather that this tendency represents a weakness in human nature which often plays into the hands of our adversary and against which we should be constantly on our guard.

Seekers for the pentecostal blessing sometimes seem so taken with the prolonged waiting in prayer, the sound as of the rushing of a mighty wind (a truly awesome thing), tongues parting asunder like as of fire, Galilean peasants speaking the mighty works of God in other languages than their own—so taken, I say, with these strange phenomena that they entirely miss the central fact. These are tremendous portents at which we cannot cease to marvel, but they pertain to the outer realm of circumstance. They are not the essence. The simple and essential fact is that the Comforter has come.

The story of our Saviour's birth is an apt illustration of this point. His advent also was marked by signal tokens. One can but wonder at the appearance of the angels to the shepherds and the melody of their song which floated out on the quiet Judean hills that night when Jesus was born. Fascinating beyond words are the Wise Men from the East and the star that so peculiarly guided their quest to the Christ child. But the great central fact to lay hold upon is that the promised Messiah had come. "The Word became flesh and dwelt among us" (John 1:14). It is even so with the third person of the Trinity.

According to promise, he had come to dwell in a new way in the hearts of all believers. The signs of Pentecost were the mighty declaration that God had done all that he had promised. He had poured forth of his Spirit upon all flesh. Through his indwelling power there was now available for all men everywhere a life of unbroken communion with the Father and with the Son, a life of victory and joy unspeakable.

THE PROMISE APPROPRIATED

After a promise has been made and fulfilled, there still remains the matter of its appropriation. What else is there to do? And yet, well-meaning, hungry-hearted people are continually trying to do something else by this promise of Pentecost. They try and fall back in disappointment and defeat. Apparently they are prepared to go to any length of endeavor, to say or do anything except the *one* thing necessary—to appropriate it as a simple act of faith.

From the nature of the case the remainder of this chapter must take the form of a personal testimony. The truth that I seek to impart came to me through experience, and I know no better way to pass it on than to share that experience with my readers.

It was precisely in this matter of appropriation that I had my difficulty. My question was, "How can I enjoy this blessing of Pentecost?" I wanted what the apostles and the early Christians had. I wanted nothing less than to be filled with the Spirit, and I felt somehow that I was prepared to go to any length to get it. But *how?* There seemed to be confusion as I sought the answer to my question, both in the testimony of Scripture and in the testimony of those qualified to speak from experience in such matters. I longed for a formula—steps, one, two, three—and lo, it's mine! But the answer did not come in this way. Somehow the Spirit of God has been careful in answering my question to avoid any resemblance to a formula. He refuses to be bound, even by his own precedent, and remains free as the wind that blows to act in sovereign grace.

Some passages of Scripture seemed to teach that the gift of the Spirit was made to all true believers in Jesus. First Corinthians 6:19 was especially clear. "Know ye not that your body is a temple of the Holy Spirit which is in you, which ye have from God?" The saints addressed in that passage were very much like ourselves, certainly far from perfect. Yet Paul taught that the Holy Spirit was in them, and the reminder of his presence was to spur them to nobler living. John 7:39 also indicated that the Holy Spirit was to be a gift to all who believed on Jesus. "But this he spake of the Spirit which they that believed on him were to receive." Receiving him was apparently the natural consequence of faith in Jesus. In another passage the American Revised Version makes clear the same meaning, especially when contrasted with the King James Version. "Did ye receive the Holy Spirit when ye believed?" (Acts 19:2); rather than, "Have ye received the Holy Ghost *since* ye believed?" The very promise of Pentecost was yet another case in point. Peter, I noted, did not say to his inquirers, "What do you expect? We tarried here for ten days in agonizing prayer. After you go through a similar experience of preparation maybe you can come into a like blessing." Instead, he said, "Repent"—deal faithfully with the sin question—"and ye shall recieve the gift of the Holy Spirit, for to you is the promise" (Acts 2:38–39).

Such passages as these found support in the teachings of some whose experience in such matters I had come to respect. I was especially impressed that James S. McConkey set forth essentially this idea.[5] I came to feel that God, who spared not his Son but freely delivered him up for us all, surely would not withhold his Spirit from us but would give him just as freely. It seemed just a matter of recognizing his presence within and yielding to him.

But that did not satisfy. I was haunted by other passages which seemed to teach that after believing on Jesus there was yet some subsequent work of grace through which the Spirit came in cleansing, sanctifying power. The converts of Samaria, I recalled, believed Philip, who proclaimed unto them the Christ. But after Peter and John came from

[5] James S. McConkey, *The Three-fold Secret of the Holy Spirit* (Harrisburg: F. Kelker, 1897).

Jerusalem and prayed and laid their hands on them, they were filled with the Holy Spirit and spake with tongues. Earnestly I wished that they might lay their hands on me! Paul dealt with the disciples of John in such a way that when he also "had laid his hands upon them, the Holy Spirit came upon them; and they spake with tongues, and prophesied" (Acts 19:6).

Supporting these passages were the testimonies of great and good men like Finney, on whom the Spirit of God came in mighty power. Some of my missionary friends brought glowing accounts from the revival at that time in North China. They spoke of the difference among the Christians before and after their "baptism." Their experience seemed to indicate that one must seek for the baptism of the Spirit, tarrying and agonizing until the mighty works of another Pentecost gave evidence of the Spirit's presence in power.

I was willing to ask, to seek, to agonize, but for what? Had I the right to insist that my experience with the Spirit be like this person's or another's? I had not done so with the Saviour when he saved me. Should I prescribe now the way in which the Spirit was to come upon me? I thought not, but I wanted to be sure. I was in a place of responsibility. What must I tell others who were seeking? In desperation I went to God with my problem. I was in earnest and there came a boldness in my praying. I asked him to tell me for my own sake and for the sake of others who looked to me for leadership. I told him I felt that I had a right to know, and that I was asking him now even as the disciples of old used to ask the Master about things which perplexed them. I asked in faith, believing that the Holy Spirit would give me a satisfying answer.

And this he did in quite a simple way, recalling a story buried deep in my subconscious mind. It is wonderful how he brings things to remembrance and applies them to our need. So far as the story itself is concerned I cannot vouch for its details and its accuracy; I want only to get across the idea that was given to me through this medium.

This is the story: Many years ago there was to be a wedding between two very prominent families. Wealth and social distinction were on both sides of the match, and it was natural that the event should assume proportions of the first magnitude. Elaborate preparations were made. The minister who was to perform the ceremony and his wife were greatly interested, of course, and would have been less than human if they had not speculated between themselves what the fee might be. Maybe the minister's wife, who according to a custom of long standing lays claim to the wedding fee, was thinking in terms of a new bonnet!

However, when the ceremony was over the groom presented the minister with a pair of kid gloves as a token of his appreciation. The preacher took them home, and with a laugh tossed them into his wife's lap saying, "There's your wedding fee." They laughed together, for obviously the gloves were too large for her and he was not the glove-wearing kind. Thus, the incident passed.

Some months later, however, as he was packing for a trip, his wife suggested that he ought to take the gloves. He might want to wear them amid his new surroundings. Thinking well of the idea he tried them on for the first time. To his surprise he found something lodged in one of the fingers of the glove. Pulling it out, he discovered a neatly folded ten-dollar bill. In the second finger he found another. Then excitedly he and his wife went through the fingers and thumbs of the gloves, finding in each a crisp ten-dollar bill—a handsome fee of one hundred dollars!

This is the story the Spirit called to mind, and I saw the point, as you do, in a flash. The gift of one hundred dollars was made and received at the time of the wedding. One could truthfully say that the groom had given his pastor the fee and that the pastor had accepted it. The money might well have been discovered at the time. The full significance of the gift, however, was unappreciated and unused until a sense of need led the preacher to an act of appropriation in which the groom's generosity was realized—and then not all at once, but in ten successive discoveries. Just so, when the believer accepts Christ, he accepts God's all—the Spirit included. It may be, as in the case of Cornelius, that the full realization of this wonderful gift comes at the moment of belief. That is the ideal way. But more often the discovery comes later—sometimes all at once, and sometimes in successive experiences, but always when there has been a sense of need deep enough to prompt a fresh appropriation.

The wonderful thing about this story is that it checks with experience. When someone has received a "baptism" of the Spirit and has been transported by attendant ecstasy, I rejoice with him. Some people are saved in a spectacular manner, and I rejoice in that also. In my own case, my experience with Jesus was very quiet. But it was none the less real for that reason. It was that way, too, when the Holy Spirit came with a new meaning into my life. I can quite easily understand why this fresh discovery of the Spirit should be so spectacular to some that they describe it as a "second work of grace." That is not the term I would use, for there have been many subsequent needs and appropriations, each different from the other, and all precious beyond words to describe.

After all, it is no claim to any merit of my own that I have received the gift of God's Son as my Saviour and Lord. I feel that I boast no righteousness to state simply that I have received as freely the gift of God's Holy Spirit as my Comforter and ever-present Friend. It is as possible and as natural to do business with the Spirit as with the Son. In either case one acts in simple faith. My justification rests on a person-to-person experience with Jesus the Saviour; in like manner my sanctification rests on a person-to-person experience with the Spirit of God. It is no longer a question of how fully do I possess the Spirit, but rather how fully does the Spirit possess me. I have learned that the Holy Spirit means what he says and that I can trust him completely. It is a joy to do business with him. I long to be his, and he knows it. He is more anxious to make me so than I can possibly be. When I trust him to take possession, I can be sure that he will do it. Results and attendant circumstances I leave with him, fully assured that now, because I am his, he also is mine. And since all this has taken place, life has been, if not spectacularly different overnight, increasingly so over the years, with mountain-top experiences now and again known only to God and myself. And if I understand the promise of Pentecost, the best is yet to be.